THE TRINITY

Scripture Testimony to the One Eternal Godhead
of the Father, and of the Son,
and of the Holy Spirit

by

EDWARD HENRY BICKERSTETH

Companion volume to "THE HOLY SPIRIT"

KREGEL PUBLICATIONS
Grand Rapids, Michigan 49501

Library of Congress Catalog Card Number 59-13770
ISBN 0-8254-2226-4

The Trinity by Edward Henry Bickersteth was originally published as *The Rock of Ages, or Three Persons But One God.* This edition, complete and unabridged, published by Kregel Publications, a division of Kregel, Inc., P.O. Box 2607, Grand Rapids, Michigan 49501. All rights reserved.

Reprinted 1957
Second Printing....................1959
Third Printing 1965
Fourth Printing 1969
Fifth Printing 1973
New Paperback Edition 1976

FOREWORD

Much confusion exists in the minds of God's people concerning the Trinity of heaven, the Father, the Son, and the Spirit. Some believe that they are three aspects of just one Person. This they illustrate by speaking of the sun as having light, heat and power. Others think that there is only one Person who is God, and that Person is the Lord Jesus, and that no other Person will be seen on the Throne in heaven but the Son. There are others who believe that God is a Person who manifests Himself sometimes as Jesus, and sometimes as the Spirit, and eventually as the Father.

Dr. Bickersteth has presented in a wonderful way a multitude of Scripture texts which correct the thinking, and make clear the true nature of the Trinity. In some cases he presents in parallel columns that which is said of each separate Person of the Trinity, so that it may be clearly seen that there are three distinct and definite Persons who are in this holy Trinity, and whom we call the God-head. He finds the truth concerning the Trinity in many passages of the Old Testament, which otherwise would be most difficult to understand. He has carefully presented the various attributes and activities of each Person of the heavenly Trinity, so that the mind will not be confused when reading these passages.

Bible students will find a wealth of information and inspiration in this volume, for each Person of the Trinity is presented in clear, unmistakeable terms for our hearts' affections. He especially stresses the fact that the term "God" refers to each Person of the Trinity, and does not always refer to the Father. He shows that the word "Lord" applies to each Person of the

Trinity, and not just to the Saviour. In many passages where the text does not clearly reveal which Person of the Trinity is under consideration, the author shows without question the answer to this perplexity.

We are constantly on the alert for a better knowledge of each of the Persons of the Godhead, so that these revelations will fill the heart with worship, praise and thanksgiving. The added information given us by Dr. Bickersteth in this volume will greatly add to our own efficiency in service, and holiness of living while ministering to others.

This book has had that effect in my own heart and life. As you read this marvelous unfolding of the personality of each of these great Three you will be led to worship God as you never did before.

WALTER L. WILSON. M.D., D.D., L.H.D.
Kansas City, Missouri

PREFACE

THE title-page of this Treatise may sufficiently indicate the line of argument I have attempted to pursue. My standard of reference throughout has been the memorable precept, "Trust ye in the Lord for ever, for in the Lord Jehovah is the Rock of Ages." (Isai. xxvi. 4.) That the one Infinite God claims our supreme and undivided confidence; that the same confidence is, on the warrant of Scripture, to be reposed in the Father, and in the Son, and in the Holy Ghost; and that therefore Father, Son, and Spirit, are equally God over all, blessed for ever, the Triune Jehovah, in whose name alone we trust, on whose arm we rely, and whose majesty alone we adore and love:—such is the brief outline of a train of thought indelibly impressed many years ago on my own mind.

Local circumstances, to which I allude in my opening chapter, induced me lately to commit these thoughts to paper. I intended to write only a brief pamphlet. But I found that proofs from the written word accumulated upon me so rapidly, that I could not duly sketch this most momentous of subjects in so cursory a way. I therefore suffered Scripture as it were to lead me by the hand; until, by compiling and illustrating Bible

evidence alone, my little essay swelled to nearly its present dimensions. And, when the rough draught of my manuscript
was to some extent completed, I did not scruple to avail myself
of the labours of those authors, to which I have from time to
time referred, so far as my limited leisure permitted me to consult them. I especially allude to Dr. Pye Smith's "Scripture
Testimony to the Messiah:" my readers will find how much I
am indebted to that truly learned and elaborate work. I would
also mention a short but valuable treatise, now out of print, by
the late Mr. Serjeant Sellon; Dwight's Theology, vol. ii.;
Wardlaw's Discourses; Serle's Horae Solitariae; Lectures at
Christ's Church, Liverpool; Scholefield's Hints; Dr. Gordon's
Supreme Godhead of Christ; and Jones's Catholic Doctrine of
a Trinity: though to many of these authors I have only been
able to refer, as isolated passages led me to desire to know
their judgment on contested interpretations. And here I cannot refrain from expressing my grateful obligations to my
learned and judicious friend, the Rev. John Ayre, who most
kindly looked through the proof-sheets of the first edition, and
gave me, on several difficult passages of Scripture, the benefit
of his extensive reading. With respect to the last mentioned
book, "Jones's Catholic Doctrine," which contains so much in
so brief a space, I had not seen it until my treatise was almost
finished. His system of proof is in some respects similar to
mine: but even my threefold comparison in the last chapter of
this work, which resembles his arrangement the nearest, was
commenced before the possession of his work enabled me to en-
rich this, and two or three earlier sections likewise, with some
most apposite quotations gleaned by him from the word of God.
I mention this only to show that my collection of Scriptural

evidence was, in the main, independent; for in such a subject, of all others, claims of originality can have no place. Here eminently κοίνα τὰ τῶν ψίλων. But while speaking of other writers, may I be permitted to urge any, who do not know them, to study some essays "On the Religions of Man and the Religion of God," by the late Professor Vinet, of Lausanne? Space alone prevented my quoting at the close of this book, a large portion of his admirable remarks on the mysteries of Christianity. He is not unjustly called the Chalmers of Switzerland.

But after all, our appeal must be to *One Book*. I have honestly tried to understand the views of sincere Unitarians; but I can come to no other conclusion, than that, while sometimes freely using the language of Scripture with respect to our Lord, they regard him only as a most highly exalted and divinely endowed CREATURE. In a word, to them he is not God. And therefore, on their hypothesis, if men trust in him for eternal salvation, reposing their entire confidence in him, they are trusting in a creature, which is idolatry. (Jer. xvii. 5—8. Whereas if they do not so trust in him, they are rejecting the only name under heaven given among men whereby we must be saved. (Acts iv. 12.) From this disastrous alternative, I see no possible escape.

I rejoice to think, however, they are bound down by no definite creed of error. They are, to use their own emphatic expression, "a drifting body." Oh that it might please God that the movement amongst the American Unitarians might spread to our own land! And whilst they profess to draw their faith from the oracles of truth, who can despair of their being brought back to the one flock, and the one Shepherd? For "the law of the Lord is perfect, converting the soul;" "the

entrance of thy words giveth light;" "the sword of the Spirit
is the word of God." In the humble hope that some may be
led to search anew, and to believe at last the Scriptures which
testify of Jesus, these pages have been written; and utterly
disclaiming all confidence in any other weapons, my one prayer
is that the Divine Spirit may cast down imaginations and every
high thing that exalteth itself against the knowledge of God,
and may bring into captivity every thought to the obedience of
Christ.

CHRIST CHURCH PARSONAGE, HAMPSTEAD.

CONTENTS

CHAPTER I.—Introduction. Preparation of heart. Our position before God. p. 9—16.

CHAPTER II.—That Scripture, in the Old and the New Testament alike, detaches our ultimate confidence from man the creature, and attaches it to God the Creator;—
by contrasting the sinfulness and feebleness of mortal man with the goodness and omnipotence of the Eternal Jehovah:
by direct prohibition and precept:
by exhibiting the holy jealousy of God. p. 17—23.

CHAPTER III.—That Scripture, in the Old and the New Testament alike, requires us to repose our ultimate confidence in the Lord Jesus Christ:
as One who is distinct from the Father:
as One to whom all the attributes of essential Deity are ascribed,
as One whose infinite perfections claim supreme trust, adoration: and love. p. 24—38.

CHAPTER IV.—That Scripture, in the Old and the New Testament alikel proves the coequal Deity of Jesus Christ with that of the eterna, Father;—
by a comparison of the attributes, the majesty and the claims of the Father and the Son:
by the appearances of God to the Old Testament saints;
by the direct and Divine worship paid to Christ:
by the conjunction of the Father and the Son in Divine offices:
by explicit assertions that Christ is Jehovah and God. p. 38—90.

CHAPTER V.—That Scripture, in the Old and the New Testament alike, presents to us the incarnation and the mission of the Saviour, as the extremity of condescension in Jehovah, that thereby he might exalt us to everlasting life.

> The Scriptural order to be observed in this inquiry.
>
> The moral and spiritual majesty of the incarnation of Christ.
>
> The examination of those passages which assert his humanity by the light of others which assert his Divinity.
>
> The derived glory to which he raises believers compared with his own essential glories.   p. 90—118.

CHAPTER VI.—That Scripture, in the Old and the New Testament alike, proves the coequal Godhead of the Holy Spirit with that of the Father and of the Son:

> as One who is to be distinguished from the Father and the Son:
>
> as One to whom such personal properties and actions are assigned as prove independent and intelligent personality:
>
> as One to whom Divine attributes are ascribed and by whom Divine offices are exercised:
>
> as One worshipped in parity with the Father and the Son:
>
> as One declared to be Jehovah and God.   p. 118—143

CHAPTER VII.—That Scripture, in the Old and the New Testament alike, assures us that in the trustful knowledge of One God, the Father, the Son, and the Holy Ghost, is the spiritual life of man now and for ever.

> On the mysteries of faith.
>
> On the revealed evidences of faith.
>
> On creeds or definitions of faith.
>
> On the obedience of faith.
>
> On the full satisfaction of faith.   p. 144—176.

CHAPTER I

A DEEP conviction that many, who refuse to acknowledge the Godhead of our Lord Jesus Christ, have never duly examined one line of Scriptural argument which presents to my own mind the most conclusive evidence of this foundation truth, induces me, though "in weakness and in fear and in much trembling," to ask their patient and prayerful perusal of this Treatise. My hesitation arises not from the least doubt of the security of the doctrine, but from consciousness how unequal I am to do justice to the proofs which establish it, from a most affectionate concern for the souls of those to whom I write, and from a deep assurance that in the rejection or cordial acceptance of this truth are bound up the issues of eternal death or eternal life. _{John iii. 36; 2 John 9.}

John iii. 36; 2 John 9.

I am well aware that many larger and more elaborate treatises, written by far abler advocates, are within their reach; but sometimes, an essay written by a neighbour will be read with courteous interest when volumes of far deeper research are passed by. And my lot has been cast where many Unitarians* reside: their acts of kindness and benevolence are continually

---

* I use the word "Unitarians" as the distinctive name they have assumed; but under protest, that it does not fairly set forth the points at issue betwixt us, if for no other reason, for this, that we cleave to the Unity of God as tenaciously as they.

making themselves felt amongst us; and proofs are multiplied on every side of their own moral culture, and of their desire for the moral elevation of the poor. Who that delights in things lovely and of good report can refrain from loving their excellences? I long over them; and yet my opportunities of intercourse are of necessity casual and limited. Hence, if it will not seem presumptuous, I know not how better to account for my present address than in the language of Paul on behalf of his kinsmen, "Brethren, my heart's desire and prayer to God for Israel is, that they might be saved."

Rom. x. 1.

Another motive weighs with me; (may I ask the reader's forgiveness for any personal allusion?) but I believe few can have passed through years of more incessant spiritual conflict than myself, and this long after I had embraced the gospel with the affections of my soul. Apparent Scriptural contradictions staggered me; for I found to my cost the temptor could assail us as he assailed our Master, saying, "It is written." The battle raged over the whole field of revealed truth, though chiefly around the central fact of our holy faith, the Deity of the Son of God. The Bible was my only sword, prayer my only resource, until, through the infinite mercy of God, those very truths around which sceptical doubts had once clustered most thickly, became the strongest bulwarks, to which, when assailed on other points, I used to resort. Since that time, in the course of my ministry during the last twelve years, I have had many difficulties brought before me by Unitarians and others, but scarcely ever a perplexity which had not been suggested to my own mind, and over which I had not fought oftentimes a painful fight. So that at least I can say with Virgil's heroine,

Matt. iv. 6.

"Non ignara mali, miseris succurrere disco;"

and I can conceive no purer joy on earth than that of
being permitted to lead some other tempest-tossed spirit
to that faith, where I have found security and peace.
Those I address will at least find here no artificial
fencing, for I am no trained swordsman in this controversy; but sometimes it has pleased God to overcome
gigantic error, not by the skilful gladiator clad in the
panoply of learning, but by a few smooth stones from
the sling of a shepherd boy.

And here, if any earnest student designs to give me
his attention, I would ask him to pause, and to pour
out his heart in prayer that he may be guided into all
truth. Such an inquirer feels with me, that eternal
life is wrapped up in the knowledge of "the only true
God," and of "Jesus Christ, whom He hath sent;" John xvii. 3.
that "God is, and that he is a rewarder of them that
diligently seek him;" and will therefore feel no diffi- Heb. xi. 6.
culty in uniting with me in such or such like petitions,
every clause of which is taken from Scripture:—

"Almighty God, the God and Father of our Lord
Jesus Christ, who inhabitest eternity, who dwellest in Eph. i. 3.
the high and holy place, but with him also who is of a
contrite and humble spirit, to revive the spirit of the
humble, and to revive the heart of the contrite ones, Isai. lvii. 15.
grant me to understand the fear of the Lord, and to Prov. ii. 5.
find the knowledge of God. I cannot by searching Job xi. 7.
find out Thee unto perfection, the King eternal, im- 1 Tim. i. 17.
mortal, invisible. But look down from heaven, and
behold from the habitation of thy holiness and of thy Isai. lxiii. 15, 16.
glory. Doubtless thou art my Father. Show mercy
upon me, and be gracious unto me. Search me, O Ex. xxxiii. 19.
God, and know my heart: try me, and know my Psa. cxxxix23, 24. See mar-
thoughts, and see if there be any way of grief in me, gin.
and lead me in the way everlasting. I plead the
promise of Jesus, If ye being evil know how to give

good gifts to your children, how much more shall
Luke xi. 13. your heavenly Father give the Holy Spirit to them
that ask him? Hear me speedily, O Lord, hide not
Ps. cxliii. 7,10. thy face from me: thy Spirit is good: lead me; for
I ask in the name of Jesus, who is able to save to the
uttermost those that come unto Thee by him, seeing
Heb. vii. 25. he ever liveth to make intercession for them; and who
hath said, Whatsoever ye shall ask in my name, that
John xiv. 13. will I do, that the Father may be glorified in the Son."

Oh, solemn and blessed pursuit! We are seeking
the Lord. Strip the words, I pray you, of every un-
meaning association, and yield your whole being, understanding, heart, conscience, will, to the momentous
inquiry. Let us humble ourselves with the recollection, "Verily, thou art a God that hidest thyself, O
Isai. xlv. 15. God of Israel, the Saviour." Let us encourage ourselves with the quickly succeeding assurance, "I said
ver. 19. not unto the seed of Jacob, Seek ye me in vain." Thus,
though there will, there must be, in the self-revelation
of Him whose ways are past finding out, mysteries
beyond the reach and range of our finite capacities,
all necessary and saving knowledge is promised to the
humble student; for the words of the Psalmist have
lost nothing of their significance by the lapse of time,
"Though the Lord be high, yet hath he respect unto
Ps. cxxxviii. 6. the lowly; but the proud he knoweth afar off;" and
again, "The Lord is nigh unto them that are of a
broken heart and saveth such as be of a contrite
Ps. xxxiv. 18. spirit."

These words point to a preparation of the heart. I
ask not then, my friends, that you should inquire first
of all into the nature of God's mysterious Being, the
Deity of Jesus Christ, and the personality of the
Holy Spirit. There is a prior investigation which demands your earnest heed, and which, pursued with

prayerful study of the word of God, will, by his grace
awaken and cultivate that disposition of mind which is
fitted for the after inquiry. Starting from those truths
you acknowledge, what, I ask, is your relation to God,
what your position before him as recorded in Scripture?

You admit that God is the Supreme Creator, and
Father, and Governor, and Judge of all men. You
confess that he is infinitely holy, and just, and good.
You acknowledge that he is himself perfect love, and
must of necessity require the perfect love of his creatures for the sake of his own glory and of their hap-
piness. That grand epitome of his righteous code
of government commends itself to your inmost conscience, "Thou shalt love the Lord thy God with
all thy heart, and with all thy soul, and with all
thy strength, and with all thy mind; and thy neighbour as thyself." If you look higher than man to the Luke x. 27.
pure intelligences around the throne of glory, you can
conceive no other law binding together the perfect
society of heaven. It is the utterance of the mind of
the blessed God. But now, looking abroad as a practical and thoughtful man upon the world as it is, what
meets your eye? Selfishness, misery, discord, enmity,
rebellion; in one word, sin. Some sights of woe move
you to compassionate tears, and your heart is wrung
for the calamities of human kind; some deeds of
rapine excite in you a righteous indignation, and you
exclaim, "Such atrocities worthily deserve to be pun-
ished." You are pitiful and you are just. But remember your sense of pity and of equity is only a
faint reflection from that in the bosom of the infinite
Jehovah. His compassions fail not. His righteous- Lam. iii. 22.
ness is everlasting. He is Father, and Legislator, Ps. cxix. 142.
and Judge in one. Sin violates every obligation: it
wounds the heart of the eternal Father. Listen to

his pathetic appeal, "Hear, O heavens, and give ear,
O earth: for the Lord hath spoken, I have nourished
and brought up children, and they have rebelled
Isai. i. 2.   against me." It sets at nought the wise regulations
of the Lawgiver. He complains, "I gave them my
statutes, and showed them my judgments, which if a
man do, he shall even live in them. Notwithstanding
the children rebelled against me: they walked not in
Ezek. xx. 11, my statutes, neither kept my judgments to do them."
21.
It is provoking the judicial condemnation of Him who
now expostulates, Knowest thou not "that the goodness of God leadeth thee to repentance? but after thy
hardness and impenitent heart treasurest up unto thyself wrath against the day of wrath and revelation of
the righteous judgment of God; who will render to
Rom. ii. 4—6. every man according to his deeds."

To inquire then what is the nature of sin, its character, course, and issue, is only the part of a rational,
intelligent being. But herein, especially, it behoves
us to lay aside all prejudice and pride, to remember
how distasteful all revelations of our own corruptions
must be to the natural heart, and to reflect that the
plague, the diagnosis of which we would learn, itself
impairs our perceptive faculties. Here, then let us
Matt. xviii. 3, humble ourselves as a little child. Here, as we open
4.
the sure word of God, let us answer with Samuel of
1 Sam. iii. 9. old, "Speak, Lord; for thy servant heareth." And
here, if the probe cut deep, let us be assured, "Faithful
Prov. xxvii. 6. are the wounds of a friend," and loving is the correction of a Father who smites that he may heal and
Isai. lxi. 1.   "bind up the broken-hearted."

This evil of sin is not superficial, but radical. It
pervades human life from the cradle to the grave:
Ps. li. 5.   "Behold I was shapen in iniquity; and in sin did my
Prov. xxiv. 9. mother conceive me. The thought of foolishness is

sin. Foolishness is bound in the heart of a child. Prov. xxii. 15
The imagination of man's heart is evil from his youth. Gen. viii. 21.
The heart is deceitful above all things, and desperately Jer. xvii. 9.
wicked. From within, out of the heart of men, pro-
ceed evil thoughts . . . . all these evil things come Mark vii. 21–23.
from within, and defile the man."

This evil is not partial, but universal. None have
escaped from it. "There is not a just man upon Eccl. vii. 20.
earth, that doeth good and sinneth not. There is Rom. iii. 10.
none rightous, no, not one. All the world becomes ver. 19.
guilty before God. All have sinned, and come short ver. 23.
of the glory of God."

This evil is not self-remedial; but so far as lies in
man, incurable. "Who can bring a clean thing out of Jer. xxx. 15.
an unclean? Not one. How then can man be just Job xiv. 4.
with God? or how can he be clean that is born of a Job xxv. 4.
woman? Can the Ethiopian change his skin, or the
leopard his spots? then may ye also do good that are Jer. xiii. 23.
accustomd to do evil."

This evil is fatal. "In the day that thou eatest there- Gen. ii. 17.
of dying thou shalt die," was the warning of faithful
love to Adam, and upon the fall moral and spiritual
death marched like a pestilence through man's noble
soul. The land was as the garden of Eden before it,
and behind it a desolate wilderness. Hence disease
and decay, those symbols of a deeper malady. "And
sin, when it is finished, bringeth forth death. Death James i. 15.
passes upon all men, for that all have sinned." And to Rom. v. 12.
those who die in their sins, this death of the body is
the awful introduction of that second death, of which
the apostle writes, "Whosoever was not found written Rev. xx. 14, 15.
in the book of life was cast into the lake of fire."

Let us then return to the question, What is our own
position by nature before God? (O merciful Father,
teach me who write, and those who read, these lines to

know ourselves.) Does not that law of perfect love condemn us? does it not bring us in guilty before Him whose eyes are as a flame of fire? have not we rebelled against the majesty of Jehovah? have we not deeply wounded the paternal heart of Him who is infinite love? Alas! we have not escaped this universal corruption. We are convicts, self-condemned. We are sinners. Oh, to realize the true meaning of the word! When a man sins against his fellow, a child against his parent, a servant against his master, we appreciate the guilt. But who shall estimate the ingratitude of sin against God? All other facts are trivial compared with this—we are sinners—for sin uncleansed and unchecked is present defilement and final death.

Such is our position: a humiliating one in truth to the awakened conscience: guilty, and therefore craving pardon; weak, and therefore casting about for help; in darkness, and therefore crying out for light. What must I do to be saved? Until this is answered, every other question is a grand impertinence—saved from sin, its guilt, its power, its issue? Lord, to whom shall we go? the cry pierces heaven, and reaches the throne of the Eternal. Lord, to whom shall we go? and the response is given in the lively oracles of truth: "There is no God else beside me; a just God and a Saviour; there is none beside me. Look unto me, and be ye saved, all the ends of the earth: for I am God, and there is none else."

Isai. xlv. 21, 22.

CHAPTER II

AND this brings me to the first great proposition I would establish—

That Scripture, in the Old and the New Testament alike, detaches our ultimate confidence from man, the creature, and attaches it to God, the Creator.

This is enforced by three parallel lines of truth: (1) by contrasting the sinfulness and feebleness of mortal man with the goodness and omnipotence of the Eternal Jehovah; (2) by direct prohibition and precept; (3) by declaration of the awful jealousy of the Creator, if any creature usurp his position in our affiance and in our regard.

(1) The most casual glance at the contrast testimony of Scripture might convince us that such is the design of God.

Scripture Testimony of Man	*Scripture Testimony to God.*
1.	**1.**
We are but of yesterday, and know nothing, because our days upon earth are a shadow.—*Job* viii. 9.	Thou art from everlasting.—*Ps.* xciii. 2. All things naked to his eyes.—*Heb.* iv. 13. He inhabiteth eternity.—*Isai.* lvii. 15.
2.	**2.**
Ye are not able to do that thing which is least.—*Luke* xii. 26.	With God all things are possible.—*Matt.* xix. 26.
3.	**3.**
How much less in them that dwell in houses of clay, whose foundation is in the dust, which are crushed before the moth.—*Job* iv. 19.	The heaven of heavens cannot contain thee.—1 *Kings* viii. 27. God is a Spirit.—*John* iv. 24. The Lord God omnipotent.—*Rev.* xix. 6.
4.	**4.**
The thoughts of man—are vanity.—*Psalm* xciv. 11.	The counsel of Jehovah standeth for ever: the thoughts of his heart to all generations.—*Psalm* xxxiii. 11.

Scripture Testimony of Man.	*Scripture Testimony to God.*
He turneth wise men backward, and maketh their knowledge foolish. —*Isai.* xliv. 25.	The immutability of his counsel.— *Heb.* vi. 17.
5.	5.
All flesh is grass, and all the goodliness thereof is as the flower of the field.—*Isai.* xl. 6.	The eternal God.—*Deut.* xxxiii. 27. The glory of Jehovah shall endure for ever.—*Psalm* civ. 31.
6.	6.
There is none righteous, no, not one.— *Rom.* iii. 10.	There is none good but one, that is, God.—*Matt.* xix. 17.
7.	7.
The heart is deceitful above all things, and desperately wicked: who can know it?—*Jer.* xvii. 9. Man looketh on the outward appearance.—1 *Sam.* xvi. 7.	God is light, and in him is no darkness at all.—1 *John* i. 5. I the Lord search the heart.—*Jer.* xvii. 10. But the Lord looketh on the heart.— 1 *Sam.* xvi. 7.
8.	8.
A man that shall die.—*Isai.* li. 12.	Who only hath immortality.—1 *Tim.* vi. 16.
9.	9.
In Him we live, and move, and have our being.—*Acts* xvii. 28.	The Father hath life in himself.—*John* v. 26.
10.	10.
Woe unto him that striveth with his Maker! Shall the clay say to him that fashioneth it, What makest thou?—*Isai.* xlv. 9.	I have made the earth, and created man upon it.—*Isai.* xlv. 12. He fashioneth the hearts (of the sons of men) alike.—*Psalm* xxxiii. 15.

Chap. II.   This testimony might be almost indefinitely prolonged: the above may suffice. But I would venture to draw your attention to three or four passages, where the contrast is forced upon our notice by the sacred writer himself.

If, for example, we turn to the prayer of Moses, he reposes supreme trust in the Eternal: "Lord, thou hast been our dwelling-place in all generations. Before the mountains were brought forth, or ever thou hadst formed the earth and the world, even from everlasting

CHAP. II.

Psa. xc. 1, 2.

to everlasting, thou art God;" and contrasts this im-
mutability of the Most High with the brief life of men:
"They are as a sleep: in the morning they are like
grass which groweth up. In the morning it flourish-
eth, and groweth up; in the evening it is cut down,
and withereth."* This was the lesson so often and so
painfully taught to Israel of old, by a Father's solemn
chastisements and forgiving love. From frequent
expostulations I select one:—"Woe to them that go
down to Egypt for help; and stay on horses, and trust
in chariots, because they are many; and in horsemen,
because they are very strong; but they look not unto
the Holy One of Israel, neither seek the Lord." And
what is the reason given? "Now the Egyptians are
men, and not God; and their horses flesh, and not
Spirit." And what is the urgent entreaty founded
thereon? "Turn ye unto Him from whom the children of Israel have deeply revolted." Again, this
message is sent to captive Zion: "I, even I, am He
that comforteth you: who art thou, that thou
shouldest be afraid of a man that shall die, and of the
son of man which shall be made as grass; and forget-
test the Lord thy Maker, that hath stretched forth the
heavens, and laid the foundations of the earth?" Observe, in all these passages, how much stress is laid on
the creative power of God as proof of his infinite pre-
eminence. The Maker alone is mighty to save. And
if it be so in temporal deliverances, how much more
in respect of that eternal salvation which must engross
the regards of every thoughtful man, seeing that the
Psalmist says of the rich men of earth, "None of them

ver. 5, 6.

Isai. xxxi. 1.

ver. 3.

ver. 6.

Isai. li. 12, 13.
See ver. 15.

---

* I would pray the reader to compare the way in which this
same figure, this parable to all nations, is enlarged upon in Isaiah
xl. 6—8, and is enforced in the New Testament, 1 Pet. i. 24;
James i. 10, 11.

Psa. xlix. 7, 8.

ver. 15.

Ps. cxlvi. 3–6.

Isai. ii. 22.

1 Pet. i. 21.

Ex. xxxiv. 14.

can by any means redeem his brother, nor give to God a ransom for him,—for the redemption of their soul is precious!" "But God," as he shortly after cries in the rebounding exultation of faith, "God will redeem my soul from the power of the grave; for he shall receive me."

(2) Furthermore, the prohibitions and precepts are direct and express. "Put not your trust in princes, nor in the son of man, in whom there is no help. His breath goeth forth, he returneth to his earth; in that very day his thoughts perish. Happy is he that hath the God of Jacob for his help, whose hope is in the Lord his God: which made heaven, and earth, the sea, and all that therein is: which keepeth truth for ever." So again, Isaiah, having spoken of the fear of the Lord and of the glory of his majesty, says, "Cease ye from man, whose breath is in his nostrils: for wherein is he to be accounted of?" I need not multiply passages to prove that the explicit commands of Scripture with one consentient voice require, in the words of Peter, that our "faith and hope be in God."

(3) But nothing can prove this fundamental truth more solemnly than the words heard by Moses on Sinai, "Thou shalt worship no other god: for the Lord, whose name is Jealous, is a jealous God." Jealousy, as usually understood, is that peculiar uneasiness which arises from the fear that another may rob us of our due honour or affection. And with fallen man towards his fallen fellows this attribute of our being, from taking an exaggerated view of our own rights and claims, from unduly depreciating those of others, and frequently from unjustly suspecting their innocent conduct, becomes the readiest vent for the outflowings of selfishness. And hence the ill name of jealousy. But not always even among

men. Thus we speak of a man, jealous for the fair
name and best interests of his friend; as Paul says
of the Corinthians, "I am jealous over you with
godly jealousy." And thus a man may be justly ^{2 Cor. xi. 2.}
jealous of his own reputation that "good name which
is rather to be chosen than great riches." In this use ^{Prov. xxii. 1.}
it is closely allied to self-respect, and springs from a
due sense of our own position and powers, of the claims
which we have upon others, and of those mutual
obligations, domestic, social, national, which lie upon
us all. Now, in a sinless world, this estimate would
be exactly true, and these requirements every moment
perfectly satisfied. But when sin breaks in, the claims
of man on man are violated; and justice, of necessity,
conceives a holy anger and a pure indignation at that
which is unjust and unequal. We see a broken fragmentary image of it in man, like the sun struggling
through mist, and reflected on agitated waters. But
in God it is without fault, or flaw, or cloud. He has
an absolutely perfect knowledge of his own supreme
majesty and goodness: he forms an absolutely perfect
estimate of the claims that supremacy has on his
creatures: and he conceives an absolutely perfect
jealousy when those obligations are set at nought.

Now, the Lord declares himself to be Self-Existent
from eternity, Omnipresent, Immutable, Almighty,
Incomprehensible, Omniscient, the Good One, the
Holy One, the Creator, Preserver, and Administrator
of all things in heaven and earth, the Searcher of
hearts, and the most high Judge of all. These attributes, indeed, would appertain to him as governing a
world which sin has never defiled, and sorrow never
darkened, and death never desolated. But when man
had broken his commands, and trodden the seductive
paths of disobedience and guilt, the Lord gives a

further and deeper revelation of his Divine goodness and grace. He reveals himself as the only Being who forgives iniquity, transgression, and sin, as the only Refuge for the fugitive, as the only Saviour, Isai. xxvi. 4. Deliverer, and Redeemer of his people.

Deut. vi. 4, 5, x. 20, 21; v. 29. Further, He claims the supreme dependence, love, worship, and service of his creatures. This you would not for a moment deny, so that you could without scruple subscribe to the language of the church of England, "My duty towards God is to believe in him, to fear him, and to love him with all my heart, with all my mind, with all my soul, and with all my strength; to worship him, to give him thanks, to put my whole trust in him; to call upon him, to honour his holy name and his word, and to serve him truly all the Church Catechism. days of my life.

But how does He regard it, if any creature usurp his rightful prerogatives, and steal away the homage of our hearts from Him who says, "I am Jehovah: that is my name; and my glory will I not give to an- Isai. xlii. 8. other?" Let me answer in the language of Scripture: —"Thus saith the Lord: Cursed be the man that trusteth in man, and maketh flesh his arm, and whose heart departeth from the Lord: for he shall be like the heath in the desert, and shall not see when good cometh; but shall inhabit the parched places in the wilderness, in a salt land and not inhabited. Blessed is the man that trusteth in the Lord, and whose hope the Lord is: for he shall be as a tree planted by the waters, and that spreadeth out her roots by the river, and shall not see when heat cometh; but her leaf shall be green; and shall not be careful in the year of Jer. xvii. 5–8. drought, neither shall cease from yielding fruit."

It is impossible in a brief treatise to exhibit the strength of this declaration. These verses do not stand isolated from the rest of Scripture. They only gather up and present to us, in a few words, its concurrent testimony from Genesis to Revelation. (O Lord, cleanse Thou the thoughts of our hearts from all creature confidence, by the inspiration of thy Holy Spirit, that we may perfectly love thee, and worthily magnify thy holy name.) For this truth stands on the fore-front of the temple of religion: "I am God, and there is none else." The dedication stone bears this golden inscription—"To the Alone, Supreme, Eternal Jehovah." And as you bow low within its holy precincts, this is the first and great commandment—"Thou shalt have none other gods but Me." And the response of every faithful worshipper is in the spirit of the Levitical adoration—"O Lord our God, blessed be thy glorious name, which is exalted above all blessing and praise. Thou, even thou, art Lord alone: thou hast made heaven, the heaven of heavens, with all their host, the earth, and all things that are therein, the seas, and all that is therein, and thou preservest them all; and the host of heaven worshippeth thee. Thou art the Lord." Such adoration as is re-echoed in the courts of heavenly glory— "Thou art worthy, O Lord, to receive glory and honour and power; for thou hast created all things, and for thy pleasure they are, and were created."

Isai. xlvi. 9.

Neh. ix. 5-6

Rev. iv. 11.

CHAPTER III

I would proceed then to my second proposition:—
That Scripture, in the Old and New Testament alike, requires us to repose our ultimate confidence in the Lord Jesus Christ.

Or in other words, I maintain that Scripture brings before us One mysterious Person, the Son of God, the Son of man, in wondrous union with the Father, but of distinct personality from the Father, to whom all the attributes of Deity are ascribed, and who claims and receives, without protest, yea, as his just and inalienable right, equal trust, adoration, love, and service, with him who says, "I am Jehovah, my Name is Jealous, and my glory will I not give to another."

If this be proved, it will appear that the dignity of Christ stands at an INFINITE distance above that of any created being whatsoever, and is ON A PERFECT LEVEL with that of the Increate Father. My whole argument indeed challenges the views of Arians as well as those of Unitarians. I am the more anxious to state this explicitly because in a most courteous answer* which has appeared to the first edition of this work, the author says—"The chief respect in which you make me feel how little insight you have into our actual position is, that you over and over again state or imply that we believe Christ to be a mere man." I had, however, guardedly stated in my preface that

---

* *Gloria Patri, by the Rev. Dr. Sadler.* I would take this opportunity of expressing my sense of the great urbanity which marks this reply; though the author has not even attempted to grapple with my main propositions, nor erected, so far as I am aware, any new defences of Unitarianism other than those which have been often proved untenable.

those whose opinions I was controverting "regarded Christ only as a most highly-exalted and divinely-endowed CREATURE: that, in a word, to them he was not God." To this I apprehend all Unitarians would subscribe. Thus Dr. Sadler quotes with approval the words, "The Father bears a likeness to the Son *whom He has created.*" And a review in "The Enquirer" of both works says,—"In Dr. Sadler's treatise there is, we need hardly observe, no attempt to retaliate the charge of idolatry, because they worship one *whom we regard as a creature.*" Now it is, in my judgment, of little moment what degree of creature-eminence you concede to the Lord Jesus, if you deny his Deity: for after all, whatever difference exists betwixt the Infinite Creator and a finite creature must still in your view exist betwixt God and Christ. But at all events, the propositions which I have drawn out on the broad basis of Scripture combat every view which denies that SUCH AS THE FATHER IS, SUCH IS THE SON, AND SUCH IS THE HOLY GHOST.

That the personality of the Father and the Son is distinct, and that they are neither to be identified nor confounded, is so self-evident a truth, and is so seldom denied by those to whom I write, that two or three Scripture proofs will abundantly suffice. At his baptism and transfiguration the voice of the Father was heard saying of him, "This is my beloved Son, in whom I am well pleased." Jesus addresses his Father in prayer. Jesus says, "It is written in your law, that the testimony of two men is true. I am one that bear witness of myself, and the Father that sent me beareth witness of me;" and further, which is incontrovertible evidence—for the will is the essence of personality—"I came down from heaven, not to do mine own will, but the will of him that sent me." But

Matt. iii. 17, and xvii. 5.

John viii. 17, 18.

John vi. 38.

the tenets of Noëtus and Sabellius, who denied this truth, are so rarely affirmed by Unitarians, that with this brief notice I may at once proceed to bring Scriptural testimony of all Divine attributes being predicated of the Son. For

Is the Father Eternal? Bethlehem was the predicted birthplace into our world, of One "whose goings forth have been from of old, from everlasting."* The Word who was made flesh and dwelt among us "was in the beginning with God:" and himself assumes the incommunicable co-eternal Name, I AM. And he, who appeared in vision to John in Patmos, like unto the Son of man, declares, "I am Alpha and Omega, the beginning and the ending, which is, and which was, and which is to come, I am the first and the last. I am he that liveth, and was dead; and, behold, I am alive for evermore. "

Micah v. 2.

John i. 2, 14.
John viii. 58.

Rev. i. 8, 11, 17, 18.
Cf. ch. ii. 8.

Compare these words, "I am the first and the last," which are here beyond contradiction uttered by the Son of man, with Isai. xliv. 6, or xlviii. 12, where the same words are confessedly used by the One Supreme God of himself, and you have, in the language of Dwight, "the strongest assertion that eternity past and to come belongs to the Son."

Is the Father Omnipresent.? Jesus says, "Where two or three are gathered together in my name, there am I in the midst of them." "There I am, not there

Matt. xviii. 20.

---

* On this passage from Micah Chrysostom observes, when contending with those who would be the first to detect any strained interpretation of their own Scriptures—Οὗτος καὶ τὴν θεότητα καὶ τὴν ἀνθρωπότητα δείκνυσι. τῷ μὲν γὰρ εἰπεῖν, αἱ ἔξοδοι αὐτοῦ ἀπ' ἀρχῆς ἐξ ἡμερῶν αἰῶνος, ΤΗΝ ΠΡΟΑΙΩΝΙΟΝ ΕΔΗΛΩΣΕΝ ΥΠΑΡΞΙΝ, κ. τ. λ. Chrysost. Contr. Jud. Op. (edit. Bened.) i. 561. The prophet here proves both the Godhead and the manhood of Christ; for in that he says, "his goings forth are from the beginning, from the days of eternity," he plainly declares his existence before all worlds, &c.

I will be, "referring to his Divine presence at all times. Two or three of his people (says Scott) may be thus met together in ten thousand places all over the earth at the same time: this must therefore be allowed to be a direct assertion of his omnipresent Deity. Again, "Lo, I am with you alway, even unto the end of the world." Is not this a positive declaration that he is ^Matt. xxviii. 20. with the apostles and succeeding ministers always unto the end of the world. But who can be so in all the separate and distinct regions in which they preached and do preach, except that Divine Being who filleth all things, that Divine Essence which occupies all space, that God who is a Spirit."*

Is the Father Immutable? "Jesus Christ is the ^Heb. xiii. 8. same yesterday, and to-day, and for ever;" and, "Unto the Son he saith,........Thou, Lord,........art ^Heb. i. 8, 10, 12. the same, and thy years shall not fail."

Is the Father Almighty? Creation demands om-

---

* Sellon's Treatise on the Deity of Christ, p. 22. The Unitarian suggestion that the end of the world signifies the end of the Jewish age, while it does not disprove the above argument, (for such unfailing presence of a mere man with his apostles in their wide-spread evangelistic labours was as impossible for forty years as for eighteen centuries,) is negatived by the only other instances of Matthew's use of this phrase (ἡ συντέλεια τοῦ αἰῶνος), ch. xiii. 39, 40, 49, where it plainly indicates the final day of judgment; and ch. xxiv. 3, where a careful consideration of the two-fold question of the disciples, founded on the two-fold declaration, ch. xxiii. 38, 39, and of the two-fold answer it receives, proves that the end of the world respects the second advent of Christ in glory. The further suggestion that the promise, "Lo, I am with you alway," was fulfilled to Paul and others by the invisible bodily presence of Christ is refuted by Peter, who says of him, "Whom the heaven must receive until the times of restitution of all things," Acts iii. 21, and by Christ Himself, who says, "And now I am no more in the world," John xvii. 11. See Dwight on this passage.

John i. 3. nipotence—"All things were made by him." The sustentation of all things demands omnipotence—
Col. i. 17. "By him all things consist." Universal government demands omnipotence—"All power is given unto
Matt. xxviii. 18. him in heaven and earth." Co-extensive operation with God the Father in a boundless empire demands omnipotence; and Jesus Christ, when explaining his words, My Father worketh hitherto and I work, declares, "What things soever He (the Father) doeth,
John v. 17–19. these also the Son doeth likewise." And a careful comparison of Rev. i. 8, with ver. 13, 17, ch. ii. 8, xxii. 13, needs, as it seems to me, leave no doubt upon our minds that the Son of man declares of himself, "I am the Almighty."

Is the Father himself incomprehensible while comprehending all things? Peter said to our Lord absolutely, without qualification, and with reference to that prerogative of omniscience, heart-knowledge,
John xxi. 17. "Lord, Thou knowest all things." And Christ Jesus says of himself, "No man knoweth the Son but the Father; neither knoweth any man the Father, save the
Matt. xi. 27. Son, and he to whomsoever the Son will reveal him." "In this passage both the omniscience and incomprehensibility of Christ are declared by himself. He who knows the Father is omniscient; he who is known
Dwight, vol. ii. 77. only by the Father is incomprehensible." Also, he
John x. 15. says, "As the Father knoweth me, even so know I the
Eph. iii. 18,19. Father." The riches of Christ are declared to be unsearchable. His love passeth knowledge. And, "In him
Col. ii. 3. are hid all the treasures of wisdom and knowledge."

Is the Father infinitely good and holy, so that
Matt. xix. 17. "there is none good but one, that is, God," and again,
1 Sam. ii. 2. "there is none holy, as Jehovah?" Jesus says, "I am the good Shepherd." And he is called, "The
Acts iii. 14, etc. Holy One and the Just—the one who knew no sin—

without sin, without spot—holy, harmless, undefiled Heb. vii. 26.
—Jesus Christ the rightcous, in whom is no sin—full
of grace and truth." John i. 14.

*Is the Father the Creator, Preserver, and Governor
of all things in heaven and earth?* Jesus is the Creator, for "by him (the Son of his love) were all things
created, that are in heaven, and that are in earth,
visible and invisible, whether they be thrones, or
dominions, or principalities, or powers: all things Col. i. 16.
were created by him and for him." And "without him
(the Word) was not even one thing made that hath John i. 3.
been made." Jesus Christ is the Preserver: for, "he
(the Son) upholds all things by the word of his power. Heb. i. 3.
In him was life; and the life was the light of men— John i. 4.
and because I live (he says), ye shall live also." Jesus John xiv. 19.
is the supreme Governor: for "unto the Son he saith,
Thy throne, O God, is for ever and ever. He is over Heb. i. 8.
all, God blessed for ever. He is King of kings, and Rom. ix. 5.
Lord of lords. And his dominion is an everlasting Rev. xix. 16.
dominion which shall not pass away, and his kingdom
that which shall not be destroyed." Dan. vii. 14;
compare also
Luke ii. 33.

Is the Father the Searcher of hearts? "These
things saith the Son of God,......all the churches
shall know that I am he which searcheth the reins and
hearts;" and "He (writes John) knew all men, and Rev. ii. 18–23.
John ii. 24, 25.
needed not that any should testify of man: for he
knew what was in man."

Is the Father the Most High Judge of all? Jesus
Christ likewise stands forth as the appointed Judge of
all men. For it is written, "We must all appear
before the judgment seat of Christ." And "when the 2 Cor. v. 10.
Son of man shall come in his glory, and all the holy
angels with him, then shall he sit upon the throne of
his glory: and before him shall be gathered all nations:
and he shall separate them one from another." Matt. xxv. 31,
32.

Here then we have all* the essential attributes of Godhead ascribed to Christ; and this, not in one or two obscure passages, but by a general consensus of those holy men who spoke as they were moved by the Holy Ghost. Many other proof texts of similar character, if space permitted, might be brought forward. But these suffice. What do you, who are seeking the Lord, learn from them of your relation to Jesus Christ? He stands forth before you, who are but of yesterday, as himself from everlasting: before you, whose life is a vapour, as having life in himself: before you, who are tied to a narrow spot of earth, as Omnipresent: before you, a mutable man, as unchangeably the same: before you, who without him can do nothing as Almighty: before you, who are not sufficient to think anything of yourself, as the Omniscient One in whom are hid all the treasures of wisdom and knowledge: before you, frail and defective, as the Holy and the Just One without sin: before you, a creature of the dust, as your Creator: before you, whose goodliness is as the flower of the field, as your Preserver: and before you, who confess your feebleness in self-government, your short-sightedness in self-knowledge, and your reliance on a court of final appeal, as the Ruler of all things, the Searcher

Job viii. 9.

John xv. 5.
2 Cor. iii. 5.

* Perhaps there is one adjective applied in Scripture to the Father, and not to the Son, I mean "*Invisible.*" If this be so, the reason is manifest from the character he sustains as the medium of communication betwixt the Creator and the creatures of his hand, "the Image of the invisible God." We have proved that he is in his Divine nature omnipresent and incomprehensible. That now we see him not, 1 Pet. i. 8, although always with us, is matter of fact. But a careful consideration of Heb. xi. 27, "he endured as seeing him that is invisible," leads me to question whether the direct reference there is not to the Word, the Angel of God's presence, first seen by Moses at the burning bush, and still visible to the eye of faith, when he braved the wrath of the king.

of all hearts, and the Judge of all men. Can it be, that, in the presence of such infinite goodness and glory, no feelings of adoration arise in your heart? It is not, that he is at an immeasurable distance from you, so that what he is and what you are, have no intimate connection. But he made you, sustains you, watches you. The offices he fills towards you are those of God. And he is so unutterably good and gracious. What remains? If you believe this testimony, you must confide in him, you must love him, you must adore him. No other feelings than those of entire reliance and supreme love would at all answer the claims of such a one upon you. And they are the Scriptures of truth which, by portraying so gracious a Lord, have elicited that confidence and warranted that affection.

But this is not all. Thus far we might argue with unfallen beings, and thus might urge those holy intelligences who left not their first estate, to obey the Divine command, "Let all the angels of God worship him." Let us remember our position before God, Heb. i. 6. fallen, guilty, strengthless, and, as reasonable beings, inquiring with the deepest anxiety, "What must I do to be saved?" Now it is not too much to say that the hopes of all mankind with regard to salvation, from the wreck of Paradise lost to the prophetic vision of Paradise restored, are fixed on this mysterious Son of man. On him, as the seed of the woman who should bruise the head of the serpent: as the Lord Gen. iii. 15. whose future advent cheered the saintly Enoch: as Jude 14. the living Redeemer on whom the patriarch Job rested his hopes of immortality: as the son of Abra- Job xix. 25. ham, a benefactor, in whom all the families of the Gen. xxii. 18. earth should be blessed: as the Shiloh of Jacob's dy- Gen. xlix. 10. ing bed: as the Angel of the burning bush and of the Exod. iii. 2; xiv. 19; fiery pillar: as the Captain who fought for Israel and xxxii. 34.

nerved the arm of her warriors: as the begotten Son

Psa. ii. 7, and cx. 1, 4. of God, the assessor of his throne, the Priest for ever, predicted by the sweet psalmist of Israel: as the

Isai. vii. 14; ix. 6. virgin-born Emmanuel, foretold by Isaiah, the Child endowed with a name of lustrous Deity, Wonderful, Counsellor, the Mighty God, the Father of eternity, the Prince of peace: as the Lord our righteousness,

Jer. xxiii. 6. anticipated by Jeremiah: as the appearance of a man

Ezek. i. 26. on the sapphire throne, seen in vision by Ezekiel: as the Messiah announced to Daniel who should be cut

Dan. ix. 24,26. off but not for himself, and should bring in everlasting righteousness; as the Desire of all nations, of

Hag. ii. 7. whom Haggai wrote: and as the Sun of righteousness, seen from afar by Malachi, who should rise on the

Mal. iv. 2. benighted world with healing in his wings:—on him, from age to age, the faith of every believer was fastened, by promise and by prophecy.

Let me, ere I pass on, select two passages from the Old Testament for your careful consideration. That same Psalm which proclaims the Divine decree— "Jehovah hath said unto me, Thou art my Son; this

Psa. ii. 7. day have I begotten thee,"—closes thus—"Kiss the Son, lest he be angry and ye perish from the way, when his wrath is kindled but a little. Blessed are all they that put their trust in him." Remember the solemn denunciation, "Cursed be the man that trust-

Jer. xvii. 5. eth in man, and maketh flesh his arm." Is there not food here for the most thoughtful inquiry? How can you reconcile these texts? I venture to assert, only in the gospel of the Son of God.

Again, if you turn to the fifty-third chapter of Isaiah, you find, "All we like sheep have gone astray;

Isai. liii. 6. we have turned every one to his own way." Comprehensive words! embracing the transgressions of six thousand years. If the sins of those many generations were gathered together, how vast the accumulation, how insufferable the load of guilt! It is done: for Scripture continues, "The Lord hath laid on (hath made to meet on) him the iniquity of us all." On *Isai. liii. 6.* him: on whom? On the chosen Servant of God in whom his soul delighteth, but whose visage is marred *Isai. xlii. 1; lii. 14.* more than any man; on one who grows up as a tender plant, who is despised and rejected of men, a man of *Isai. liii. 2, 3.* sorrows and acquainted with grief. On him, the sins of all were laid. He was wounded for our transgressions. He was bruised for our iniquities.* But can he sustain the load? Remember how earnest and awakened men would hold their breath in suspense, to catch an answer on which an immortality of weal or woe depended. Can he endure the burden? He can: he dies in the endurance. His soul is made an offering for sin. His death is swallowed up in victory. He lives. He sees his seed. The pleasure of the Lord prospers in his hand. He sees of the travail of his soul, and is satisfied—our Redeemer, our Mediator, *Isai. liii, 11.* our Advocate. I beseech you, my friends, to weigh that chapter on your knees. See you not, how the confidence of all mankind centres and clusters around that spontaneous victim, that dying man, that triumphant Saviour? The Lord grant that this same

---

* Nay more—It is, not only that he was (ver. 3) acquainted with grief, but (ver. 10) the Lord hath put him to grief: not only (ver. 5) he was bruised for our iniquities, but (ver. 10) it pleased the Lord to bruise him: not only (ver. 12) he bare the sin of many, but (ver. 6) the Lord hath laid on him the iniquity of us all: not only (ver. 7) he is brought as a lamb to the slaughter, but (ver. 10) thou shalt make his soul an offering for sin. If Jesus were only a spotless, sinless man, offering no vicarious atonement, how was it that a holy and just God—we will not say permitted such sufferings to light upon a perfectly innocent being—but himself caused him to suffer?

Scripture which was the message of life to the eunuch
Acts viii. 32–37.
of Ethiopia, may lead you to believe with all your
heart in the Deity of the Son of God.

But now let us follow the course of history. At
length the fulness of the time was come, and God sent
Gal. iv. 4.
forth his Son. Are not the eyes of all designedly
pointed to him? Angels from heaven announce the
Luke ii. 8–20.
glad tidings, Unto you is born a Saviour: simple
Matt. ii. 11.
shepherds salute him; and Eastern wise men worship
him. He grows up, as foretold, a despised Nazarene.
But, at his baptism, the heavens are opened, the Spirit
of God descends like a dove upon him, and the voice
of the Eternal Father proclaims, "This is my beloved
Matt. iii. 17.
Son, in whom I am well pleased." Soon the devil
Matt. iv. 1.
assaults him, and angels minister to him, their Lord.
His heralds points him out, "Behold the Lamb of God,
John i. 29.
which taketh away the sin of the world." He speaks
John vii. 46.
as man never spoke. He works wonders of goodness
John xv. 24.
and of grace, such as man never wrought. He intro-
duces a morality of unequalled simplicity and purity
and worth. He preaches the glad tidings of the kingdom of heaven. But his own received him not. He
is betrayed, condemned, and crucified. He dies, the
1 Pet. iii. 18.
Just for the unjust. He lays down his life. He has
John x. 18.
power to take it again. He rises. He ascends to the
Ps. lxviii. 18.
right hand of God. There he receives gifts for men.
Acts v. 31.
He sheds forth his Spirit. He gives repentance and
Heb. vii. 25.
remission of sins. He ever lives to make intercession
for us. He is preparing a place in glory for his children: and thence he shall shortly come again and take
John. xiv. 1–3.
us unto himself, that where he is there we may be also.

Who, I ask, can believe this simple story of redeeming grace, and not repose their whole confidence in
this Saviour? Who can refrain from trusting him
with supreme reliance? Who can forbear loving him

with the most absorbing love? If Scripture forbade
these emotions, as being due only to the infinite Father, what force we must lay upon ourselves to prevent
them springing up in the trustful heart! But does
Scripture forbid them? nay, verily. Prophecy, as
we have seen, foretold that thus it should be, and
blessed the confidence. And when the Saviour walked
our fallen world, suppliant sinners worship him, and
he refuses it not. They put their whole trust in him,
and he declares it not only suitable but essential. ^{John ix. 35–38.}
Upon it hangs eternity. "God so loved the world,
that he gave his only begotten Son, that whosoever believeth in him should not perish, but have everlasting
life." But is this trust altogether identical with that ^{John iii. 16.}
we are required to repose in the Father? It is one
and the same. He says, "Believe in God: believe
also in me." His invitations penetrate the weary ^{John xiv. 1.}
heart: "Come unto me, all ye that labour and are
heavy laden, and I will give you rest;" and his ^{Matt. xi. 28.}
words fall like dew on the parched and thirsty soul;
"If any man thirst, let him come unto me and drink."
He insists that "all men should honour the Son, even
as they honour the Father." He concentrates the af- ^{John v. 23.}
fection and the affiance of his people upon himself as
the one Mediator. He invites us to offer up our ^{Matt. xi. 27.}
prayers in his prevalent name. And finally, he ^{John xvi. 23, 24.}
assures us, "He gives eternal life" unto his own dis- ^{John x. 28.}
ciples, and "will raise them up at the last day." ^{John vi. 40.}

And after his ascension to glory, what is the conduct and the testimony of his chosen apostles? In
the name of Jesus Christ they do all their mighty
works. For Jesus Christ's sake they suffer the loss of
all things. They uniformly preach Jesus Christ; and
the Holy Spirit seals their message. They know no-
thing among men, but Jesus Christ and him crucified. ^{1 Cor. ii. 1–3.}

Yea, I should have to transcribe a great portion of the Epistles I wanted to transfer to these pages all the evidence those letters afford, that Scripture requires us to repose our supreme reliance on the Lord Jesus Christ. The most casual glance might make us suspect, that a name which meets our eye every few lines was none other than that of the Divine Saviour of the world. Why else its perpetual recurrence? A deeper search confirms this. Take for instance the first few verses of the Epistle to the Ephesians:—

"Paul, an apostle of Jesus Christ by the will of God, to the saints which are at Ephesus, and to the faithful in Christ Jesus: Grace be to you, and peace, from God our Father, and from the Lord Jesus Christ.

"Blessed be the God and Father of our Lord Jesus Christ, who hath blessed us with all spiritual blessings in heavenly places in Christ:

"According as He hath chosen us in him before the foundation of the world, that we should be holy and without blame before him in love:

"Having predestinated us unto the adoption of children, according to the good pleasure of his will,

"To the praise of the glory of his grace, wherein he hath made us accepted in the Beloved:

"In whom we have redemption through his blood, even the forgiveness of sins, according to the riches of his grace.".

The privileges are surpassingly great; but mark how they are all ours IN CHRIST. It is "an apostle of Jesus Christ" who writes. The church is described as the faithful "in Christ Jesus." The benediction is given from God our Father, and co-ordinately "from the Lord Jesus Christ." God is praised: it is as "the God and Father of our Lord Jesus Christ." All spiritual blessings are ours: they are ours "in Christ." We are chosen: it is "in Him." We are predestinated unto the adoption of children: it is "by Jesus

Christ." We are accepted: it is "in the Beloved."
We have redemption, even the forgiveness of sins: it
is "in him through his blood." We are indebted to
Christ for all. We are compelled to look up into
him, and say—"O Lord, my trust is in thee."

The force of this reasoning will appear more strongly
if you attempt to substitute here for the name of Jesus
that of any man, however exalted and self-devoted, or
of any creature, however lofty in the scale of creation.
Make the trial. Read the passage given above, sub-
stituting the name of Michael the archangel, or of
Moses the legal mediator, or of Stephen who sealed
his witness with his blood, for that only "name under
heaven given among men, whereby we must be saved." Acts iv. 12.
You cannot do it. You stop short. It is an intoler-
able discord. It is blasphemy. For you feel this
would be reposing in the creature an exhaustive confidence due only to the Infinite Creator, and offering
to man a supreme gratitude which is the prerogative
of God our Saviour.

Such passages might be easily multiplied. I would
mention the first chapters of the Epistle to the Colos-
sians, of Peter's first Epistle, of John's first Epistle:
—I study all, and in all I find Jesus my Saviour. Do you admit the cry of the awakened conscience is, "What must I do to be saved?" You
must acknowledge that the reply of the New Testament from end to end,—from the angel's message to
Joseph, "Thou shalt call his name Jesus: for he shall
save his people from their sins," to the ascription of Matt. i. 21.
praise recorded by the aged John in Patmos, "Unto
him that loved us, and washed us from our sins in his
own blood, and hath made us kings and priests unto
God and his Father"—the reply, I say, is plain and
unhesitating, "Believe on the Lord Jesus Christ, and

Acts xvi. 31.

thou shalt be saved." It is not only that one of illimitable goodness and infinite perfections, your Creator and Preserver, stands before you, a man of limited
and finite capacities: but he presents himself to you
fallen, and guilty, and lost, as one who is able and
willing to raise you from the lowest depths of sin and
make you members of a royal priesthood, and cause
you to reign with him among the sons of light for
ever and for ever. No utterance but one like Mary's
satisfies his claims: "My spirit hath rejoiced in God

Luke i. 47

my Saviour." The Lord grant unto you and me like
precious faith, that resting on these exceeding great

2 Pet. i. 1, 4,
11.

and precious promises, an entrance may be ministered
unto us into the everlasting kingdom of our Lord and
Saviour Jesus Christ!

CHAPTER IV

Chap. IV.

THE preceding truths will have prepared the way
for my third proposition:—

*That Scripture, in the Old and the New Testament
alike, proves the co-equal Deity of Jesus Christ with
that of the Eternal Father:*

by a comparison of the attributes, the majesty, and
the claims of the Father and the Son;
by the appearances of God to the Old Testament
saints;
by the direct and Divine worship paid to Christ;
by the conjunction of the Father and the Son in
Divine offices:
by explicit assertions that Christ is Jehovah and God.

And here I would ask your further honest application
of that great principle of heavenly scholarship, "the

comparing spiritual things with spiritual." For just
as in algebra, from the combination of two known
quantities the unknown is found out; as in trigonometry, if out of the six parts of a triangle any three, one
being a side, are given, the others are discoverable,
from which simple law have resulted all the triumphs
of astronomy; so, in searching the Scriptures, those
humble students, who prayerfully compare and com-
bine them, shall know "the things that are freely
given to us of God."

1 Cor. ii. 12, 13.

(1.) I would first then place side by side the witness
of Scripture to the attributes, the majesty, and the
claims of the Father and the Son. Only a selection
from the abundant materials could of course be made.
I have exercised a rigid caution in the verses adduced
in testimony of Christ, setting many aside which I
fully believe bear witness of him. But, if after candid
investigation you think one, or more than one, inapplicable to the Messiah, I pray you draw your pencil
through those, which may seem to you even ambiguous.
Sufficient, and more than sufficient, will, I am persuaded, remain uncancelled. Some marked with an
asterisk are discussed or illustrated in other portions
of this treatise, and will be easily found by a reference
to the Scripture Index at the close. In some of the
passages in the left hand column, I believe the *primary*
reference to be not to the Father but to the Son; but
this does not invalidate the testimony to be derived
from them, as in every case the witness is said to be
of God, or of the Lord Jehovah; and no one, who denied the Deity of Christ, could maintain, that a single
passage there adduced designates the Messiah, without
contradicting himself. I earnestly ask your calm,
dispassionate collation of these passages: and I pray
you, whilst you proceed, to suffer the full weight of

Isai. xlii. 8.

these solemn words to rest upon your mind and memory, "I am Jehovah—that is my name: and my glory will I not give to another."

Scripture Testimony to God the Father, or to God absolutely.	*Scripture Testimony to Christ.*
1.	1.
From everlasting to everlasting, thou art God.—*Psalm* xc. 2.	Whose goings forth have been from of old, from everlasting.—*Mic.* v. 2.
Thy throne is established of old: thou art from everlasting.—*Psalm* xciii. 2.	Unto the Son he saith, Thy throne, O God, is for ever and ever.— *Heb.* i. 8.
I am the first, and I am the last; and besides me there is no God.—*Isai.* xliv. 6.	I am the first and the last: I am he that liveth and was dead.—*Rev.* i. 17, 18.
2.	2.
Do not I fill heaven and earth? saith the Lord.—*Jer.* xxiii. 24.	He that descended is the same also that ascended up far above all heavens, that he might fill all things.*— *Eph.* iv. 10.
The Lord, he it is that doth go before thee—He will be with thee; he will not fail thee.—*Deut.* xxxi. 8.	*Lo, I am with you alway, even unto the end of the world.—*Matt.* xxviii. 20.
3.	3.
I am Jehovah, I change not.—*Malachi* iii. 6.	Jesus Christ, the same yesterday, to-day, and for ever.—*Heb.* xiii. 8.
4.	4.
I am the Almighty God.—*Gen.* xvii. 1.	*I am....the Almighty.—*Rev.* i. 8.
Whatsoever the Lord pleased, that did	Whatsoever things he doeth, these

---

* It has been objected that "the filling all things," in Ephesians iv. 10, refers not to the occupation of space, but to pre-eminence of dignity. But we must interpret the words of Jeremiah by the true definition of omnipresence, namely, not that God is present in everything, but that all things are present to God, and this God present everywhere: as in Newton's well-known words respecting the Deity. "Aeternus est et infinitus, omnipotens et omnisciens; id est, durat ab aeterno in aeternum, et adest ab infinito ad infinitum. Non est aeternitas et infinitas, sed aeternus et infinitus; non est duratio et spatium, sed durat et adest, durat semper et adest ubique." Bearing this in mind, I see no meaning to be attached to the words of the prophet regarding Jehovah, which you must not also attach to the words of the apostle regarding Christ.

Scripture Testimony to God the Father, or to God absolutely.	Scripture Testimony to Christ.
he in heaven and in earth.—*Ps.* cxxxv. 6.	also doeth the Son likewise.—*John* v. 19.
5.	5.
Canst thou by searching find out God? —*Job.* xi. 7.	No man knoweth the Son, but the Father.—*Matt.* xi. 27.
As the Father knoweth me.—*John* x. 15.	Even so know I the Father.—*John* x. 15.
O the depth of the riches both of the wisdom and knowledge of God! his ways past finding out (ἀνεξιχνίαστοι, trackless).—*Rom.* xi. 33.	The unsearchable (ἀνεξιχνίαστον) riches of Christ.—*Eph.* iii. 8.
Thy footsteps (τὰ ἴχνη σου—*LXX.*) are not known.—*Psalm* lxxvii. 19.	The love of Christ, which passeth knowledge.—*Eph.* iii. 19.
6.	6.
I am Jehovah thy God, the Holy One (ὁ ἅγιος—*LXX.*) of Israel.—*Isai.* xliii. 3.	Ye denied the Holy One (τὸν ἅγιον) and the Just.—*Acts* iii. 14.
A God of truth and without iniquity. —*Deut.* xxxii. 4.	I am...the Truth.—*John* xiv. 6. Without sin.—*Heb.* iv. 15.
7.	7.
In the beginning God created the heavens and the earth.—*Gen.* i. 1.	In the beginning was the Word. All things were made by him.—*John* i. 1; 3.
I am Jehovah, that maketh all things; that stretcheth forth the heavens alone; that spreadeth abroad the earth by myself.—*Isai.* xliv. 24.	By him were all things created, that are in heaven, and that are in earth, visible and invisible, whether they be thrones, or dominions, or principalities, or powers:
The Lord hath made all things for himself.—*Prov.* xvi. 4.	All things were created by him, and for him.—*Col.* i. 16.
8.	8.
Thou preservest them all.—*Neh.* ix. 6. In him we live.—*Acts* xvii. 28.	By him all things consist.—*Col.* i. 17. Because I live, ye shall live also.—*John* xiv. 19.
9.	9.
The King of kings, and Lord of lords. —1 *Tim.* vi. 15.	King of kings, and Lord of lords.— *Rev.* xix. 16.
Thy kingdom is an everlasting kingdom, and thy dominion endureth throughout all generations.—*Psalm* cxlv. 13.	His dominion is an everlasting dominion . . . . and his kingdom that which shall not be destroyed.— *Dan.* vii. 14.

Scripture Testimony to God the Father, or to God absolutely.	*Scripture Testimony to Christ.*
10.	**10.**
Thou, even thou only, knowest the hearts of all the children of men. —1 *Kings* viii. 39.	All the churches shall know that I am he which searcheth the reins and hearts.—*Rev.* ii. 23.
11.	**11.**
Shall not the Judge of all the earth do right?—*Gen.* xviii. 25.	We must all appear before the judgment seat of Christ.—2 *Cor.* v. 10.
12.	**12.**
His kingdom ruleth over all.—*Psalm* ciii. 19.	He is Lord of all.—*Acts* x. 36.
The Lord shall be king over all the earth: in that day there shall be one Lord, and his name one.— *Zech.* xiv. 9.	*To us there is but one Lord Jesus Christ, by whom are all things, and we by him.—1 *Cor.* viii. 6.
Thou, whose name alone is Jehovah, art the most high over all the earth. *Psalm* lxxxiii. 18.	God hath given him a name which is above every name.—*Phil.* ii. 9. That in all things he might have the pre-eminence.—*Col.* i. 18.
13.	**13.**
Upon the wicked he shall rain snares, fire and brimstone, and an horrible tempest.—*Psalm* xi. 6.	The Lord Jesus shall be revealed from heaven with his mighty angels, in flaming fire.
Vengeance is mine; I will repay, saith the Lord.—*Rom.* xii. 19.	Taking vengeance on them that know not God.—2 *Thess.* i. 7, 8.
The day of wrath and revelation of the righteous judgment of God.—*Rom.* ii. 5.	And from the wrath of the Lamb: for the great day of his wrath is come; and who shall be able to stand?— *Rev.* vi. 16, 17.
14.	**14.**
Behold, the Lord God will come with strong hand—His reward is with him.—*Isai.* xl. 10.	Behold, I come quickly; and my reward is with me,
Thou renderest to every man according to his work.—*Psalm* lxii. 12.	To give every man according as his work shall be.—*Rev.* xxii. 12.
15.	**15.**
To whom then will ye liken God?— *Isai.* xl. 18.	The image of the invisible God—*Col.* i. 15. The express image of his Person.— *Heb.* i. 3.
Thee the only true God (τὸν μόνον ἀλη-	* . . . . His Son Jesus Christ. This

Scripture Testimony to God the Father, or to God absolutely.	*Scripture Testimony to Christ.*
θινὸν Θεόν), [and Jesus Christ, whom thou hast sent.]—*John* xvii. 3.	(person) is the true God (οὗτός ἐστιν ὁ ἀληθινὸς Θεός) and eternal life.—1 *John* v. 20.
16.	**16.**
The Lord thy God: . . . to him shalt thou cleave.—*Deut.* x. 20.	Abide in me, and I in you. As the branch cannot bear fruit of itself;
From me is thy fruit found.—*Hosea* xiv. 8.	except it abide in the vine; no more can ye, except ye abide in me, ... for without me ye can do nothing.—*John* xv. 4, 5.
17.	**17.**
Strengthen thou me according unto thy word.—*Psalm* cxix. 28.	I can do all things through Christ which strengtheneth me.—*Phil.* iv. 13.
18.	**18.**
Lord, ... my hope is in thee.—*Psalm* xxxix. 7.	Jesus Christ, which is our hope.—1 *Tim.* i. 1.
Blessed is the man that trusteth in the Lord, and whose hope the Lord is. —*Jer.* xvii. 7.	Blessed are all they that put their trust in Him.—*Psalm* ii. 12.
	Christ in you, the hope of glory.—*Col.* i. 27.
19.	**19.**
He shall cover thee with his feathers, and under his wings shalt thou trust.—*Psalm* xci. 4.	How often would I have gathered thy children together, even as a hen gathereth her chickens under her wings.—*Matt.* xxiii. 37.
20.	**20.**
I, even I, am Jehovah; and beside me there is no Saviour.	Jesus: for he shall save his people from their sins.—*Matt.* i. 21.
—beside me no Saviour—	Christ Jesus came into the world to save sinners.—1 *Tim.* i. 15.
—beside me no Saviour—	We believe that through the grace of the Lord Jesus Christ we shall be saved.—*Acts* xv. 11.
—beside me no Saviour—	He became the Author of eternal salvation unto all them that obey him. —*Heb.* v. 9.
—beside me no Saviour—	He is able to save them to the uttermost that come unto God by Him. —*Heb.* vii. 25.

Scripture Testimony to God the Father, or to God absolutely.	*Scripture Testimony to Christ.*
—beside me no Saviour—	Jesus, which delivered us from the wrath to come.—1 *Thess.* i. 10.
—beside me no Saviour—	Our Lord and Saviour Jesus Christ.—2 *Pet.* iii. 18.
—beside me no Saviour. *Isai.* xliii. 11.	Neither is there salvation in any other; for there is none other name under heaven given among men, whereby we must be saved.—*Acts* iv. 12.
21. All flesh shall know that I the Lord am thy Saviour, And thy Redeemer, The mighty one of Jacob. *Isai.* xlix. 26.	21. *Our great God and Saviour Jesus Christ;
Let Israel hope in Jehovah . . . and he shall redeem Israel from all his iniquities (καὶ αὐτὸς λυτρώσεται τὸν Ἰσραὴλ ἐκ πασῶν τῶν ἀνομιῶν αὐτοῦ. *LXX.*)—*Psalm* cxxx. 7, 8.	Who gave himself for us, That He might redeem us from all iniquity (ἵνα λυτρώσηται ἡμᾶς ἀπὸ πάσης ἀνομίας)—*Titus* ii. 13, 14.

CHAP. IV.　　As examples of the free and unrestricted way in which the word "Saviour" is applied indiscriminately to the Father and to the Son, I would draw your attention more closely to the context of this and of two other passages in the Epistle to Titus.

1. . . . according to the commandment of God our Saviour (τοῦ σωτῆρος ἡμῶν Θεοῦ) . . . grace, mercy, and peace, from God the Father and the Lord Jesus Christ our Saviour (Χριστοῦ τοῦ σωτῆρος ἡμῶν).— Titus i. 3 4.

2. . . . . adorn the doctrine of God our Saviour (τοῦ σωτῆρος ἡμῶν Θεοῦ) in all things: for the saving (ἡ σωτήριος) grace of God hath appeared to all men— teaching us . . . that we should live . . . looking for the glorious appearing of our Great God and Saviour Jesus Christ (σωτῆρος ἡμῶν Ἰησοῦ Χριστοῦ). —Titus ii. 10—13.

3. . . . . The kindness and love towards men of God our Saviour (τοῦ σωτῆρος ἡμῶν Θεοῦ). . . . through the renewing of the Holy Ghost . . . which he shed . . . through Jesus Christ our Saviour ('Ιησοῦ Χριστοῦ τοῦ σωτῆρος ἡμῶν).—Titus iii. 4—6.

Even if you refuse to admit the simply grammatical construction of ch. ii. 13, can you believe that the name Saviour is again and again applied in a lower and subordinate sense to the Son to that it bears when applied almost in the same breath to the Father?

Scripture Testimony to God the Father, or to God absolutely.	*Scripture Testimony to Christ.*
22.	**22.**
With thee is the fountain of life: in thy light shall we see light.—*Psa.* xxxvi. 9.	In him (the Word) was life; and the life was the light of men.—*John* i. 4.
23.	**23.**
He (Jehovah of hosts) will swallow up death in victory.—*Isai.* xxv. 8.	Our Saviour Jesus Christ, who hath abolished death.—*2 Tim.* i. 10.
I will ransom them from the power of the grave; I will redeem them from death: O death, I will be thy plagues; O grave, I will be thy destruction.—*Hosea* xiii. 14.	That through death he (Jesus) might destroy him that had the power of death, that is, the devil; and deliver them who through fear of death were all their lifetime subject to bondage.—*Heb.* ii. 14, 15.

If I were to ask you to select a passage from the Old Testament, which should declare most unequivocally the supreme majesty of God, could you name a more distinctive one than the following from Isaiah? Yet illustrate this by other passages of Holy Writ, and see how all this glory appertains likewise to the only-begotten of the Father.

24.	**24.**
There is no God else beside me; A just God and a Saviour: There is none beside me.	The Word was God.—*John* i. 1. Jesus Christ the righteous: he is the propitiation for our sins.—1 *John* ii. 1, 2.

Scripture Testimony to God the Father. or to God absolutely.	*Scripture Testimony to Christ.*
Look unto me and be ye saved, All the ends of the earth: For I am God; and there is none else.	Behold the Lamb of God, which taketh away the sin of the world.—*John* i. 29.
	Every one which seeth the Son, and believeth on him, may have everlasting life.—*John* vi. 40.
I have sworn by myself, the word is gone out of my mouth in righteousness, and shall not return,	*We shall all stand at the judgment-seat of Christ. For it is written, As I live, saith the Lord, every knee shall bow to me, and every tongue shall confess to God.—*Rom.* xiv. 10, 11.
That unto me every knee shall bow, every tongue shall swear.	*In the name of Jesus every knee should bow, of things in heaven, and things in earth, and things under the earth.—*Phil.* ii. 10.
Surely, shall one say, In the Lord have I righteousness And strength:	The Branch—the Lord our righteousness.—*Jer.* xxiii, 5, 6. Without me ye can do nothing.—*John* xv. 5.
Even to him shall men come;	I will draw all men unto me.—*John* xii. 32.
And all that are incensed against him shall be ashamed.	The enemies of the cross of Christ: whose end is destruction.—*Phil.* iii. 18, 19.
In the Lord shall all the seed of Israel be justified,	He was raised again for our justification.—*Rom.* iv. 25.
And shall glory. *Isaiah* xlv. 21—25.	God forbid that I should glory, save in the cross of our Lord Jesus Christ. —*Gal.* vi. 14.

CHAP. IV.　Or if you were to choose a passage from the New Testament the most entirely devoted to the worship of the Father, you could not perhaps fix upon a more distinctive one than the Lord's prayer; in which Jesus Christ conceals his Personal glory, that as our Brother he may lead us up to the throne of grace, and cry with us, while by his Spirit he teaches us to cry, Abba, Father. Yet illustrate this by other Scriptures,

and there is no petition which might not be appropri-
ately addressed to the Son.

Scripture Testimony to God the Father, or to God absolutely.	*Scripture Testimony to Christ.*
25.	25.
Our Father which art in heaven,	The Son of man which is in heaven.—*John* iii. 13.
Hallowed be thy name.	That the name of our Lord Jesus Christ may be glorified.—2 *Thess.* i. 12.
Thy kingdom come.	The everlasting kingdom of our Lord and Saviour Jesus Christ.—2 *Pet.* i. 11.
Thy will be done in earth,	Ye serve the Lord Christ.—*Col.* iii. 24.
As it is in heaven.	Jesus Christ is gone into heaven . . . . angels and authorities and powers being made subject unto him.—1 *Pet.* iii. 22.
Give us this day our daily bread.	He shall feed his flock like a shepherd. —*Isai.* xl. 11.
Forgive us our debts, as we forgive our debtors.	Forgiving one another: even as Christ forgave you, so also do ye.—*Col.* iii. 13.
And lead us not into temptation,	He leadeth them out. My sheep . . . follow me.—*John* x. 3, 27.
but deliver us from evil:	Jesus Christ, who gave himself for our sins, that he might deliver us from this present evil world.—*Gal.* i. 4.
For thine is the kingdom, and the power, and the glory, for ever. Amen.—*Matt.* vi. 9—13.	He shall reign for ever.—*Rev.* xi. 15. To Him be glory and dominion for ever and ever. Amen.—*Rev.* i. 6.

Without denying that there is a peculiar propriety
in the offices sustained by the Father and by the Son
respectively on our behalf, these parallel passages
prove, that we may, without any impropriety, in all
the petitions which Christ has put into our lips, honour the Son even as we honour the Father.

Scripture Testimony to God the Father, or to God absolutely.	*Scripture Testimony to Christ.*
26.	**26.**
I, even I, am he that blotteth out thy transgressions for mine own sake.—*Isai.* xliii. 25.	The blood of Jesus Christ his Son cleanseth us from all sin.—1 *John* i. 7.
	When he had by himself purged our sins.—*Heb.* i. 3.
Forgiving iniquity.—*Exod.* xxxiv. 7.	Son, thy sins be forgiven thee.—*Mark* ii. 5.
27.	**27.**
Thou hast been....a refuge from the storm, a shadow from the heat.—*Isai.* xxv. 4.	A man shall be....a covert from the tempest,....as the shadow of a great rock in a weary land.—*Isai.* xxxii. 2.
He maketh the storm a calm, so that the waves thereof are still.—*Psalm* cvii. 29.	He arose, and rebuked the winds and sea; and there was a great calm. —Matt. viii. 26.
28.	**28.**
I have satiated the weary soul.—*Jer.* xxxi. 25.	Come unto me, all ye that labour,.... and ye shall find rest to your souls. —*Matt.* xi. 28, 29.
29.	**29.**
I will pour out my Spirit upon all flesh.—*Joel* ii. 28.	I will send the Comforter unto you.— *John* xvi. 7.
The Lord God, and his Spirit.—*Isai.* xlviii. 16.	Spirit of Christ.—*Rom.* viii. 9.
The Spirit of your Father.—*Matt.* x. 20.	The Spirit of his Son.—*Gal.* iv. 6.
	He hath shed forth this, which ye now see and hear.—*Acts* ii. 33.
30.	**30.**
This is the love of God, that we keep his commandments.—1 *John* v. 3.	If ye love me, keep my commandments.—*John* xiv. 15.
Thou shalt guide me with thy counsel, and afterward receive me to glory. —*Psalm* lxxiii. 24.	I will receive you unto myself.—*John* xiv. 3.
	The glory which thou gavest me I have given them.—*John* xvii. 22.
31.	**31.**
If I be a Master, where is my fear? saith the Lord of hosts.—*Mal.* i. 6.	One is your Master, even Christ.— *Matt.* xxiii. 8, 10.
Him shalt thou serve.—*Deut.* x. 20.	Ye serve the Lord Christ.—*Col.* iii. 24.

Scripture Testimony to God the Father, or to God absolutely.	*Scripture Testimony to Christ.*
32.	**32.**
Thy Maker is thine Husband: the Lord of hosts is his name.—*Isai.* liv. 5.	He that hath the bride is the Bridegroom.—*John* iii. 29. The Bride, the Lamb's wife.—*Rev.* xxi. 9.
33.	**33.**
By the grace of God I am what I am. —1 *Cor.* xv. 10. The grace of God that bringeth salvation.—*Titus* ii. 11.	Be strong in the grace that is in Christ Jesus.—2 *Tim.* ii. 1. Through the grace of the Lord Jesus Christ, we shall be saved.—*Acts* xv. 11 (quoted above.).
34.	**34.**
The love of God is shed abroad in our hearts.—*Rom.* v. 5. Alive unto God (ζῶντας τῷ Θεῷ)—*Rom.* vi. 11. Them that love God.—*Rom.* viii. 28.	The love of Christ constraineth us ....that they which live...... Should live to him that died for them (ζῶσιν τῷ ἀποθανόντι).—2 Cor. v. 14, 15. If any man love not the Lord Jesus Christ.—1 *Cor.* xvi. 22.
35.	**35.**
Thy word have I hid in mine heart.— *Psalm* cxix. 11. Thou shalt say, Thus saith the Lord God.—*Ezek.* ii. 4. [as Lawgiver: see context.]	Let the word of Christ dwell in you richly.—*Col.* iii. 16. I say unto you.—*Matt.* v. 22, 28, etc. [as Lawgiver: see context.]
36.	**36.**
Give ear, O shepherd of Israel, thou that leadest Joseph like a flock.— *Psalm* lxxx. 1. I will feed my flock, and I will cause them to lie down, saith the Lord God.—*Ezek.* xxxiv. 15. The flock of God.—1 *Peter* v. 2. I will seek that which was lost (τὸ ἀπυλωλός).—*LXX*.)—*Ezek.* xxxiv. 16. Jehovah is my Shepherd; I shall not want.	Our Lord Jesus, that great Shepherd of the sheep.—*Heb.* xiii. 20. The chief Shepherd shall appear.—1 *Peter* v. 4. I am the good Shepherd . . . there shall be one flock (ποίμνη), one shepherd.—*John* x. 14, 16. My lambs, my sheep.—*John* xxi. 15, 16. The Son of man is come to seek and to save that which was lost (τὸ ἀπωλωλός).—*Luke* xix. 10. The Shepherd . . . . of your souls.— 1 *Peter* ii. 25. My sheep shall never perish.—*John* x. 28.

7

Scripture Testimony to God the Father, or to God absolutely.	*Scripture Testimony to Christ.*
He maketh me to lie down in green pastures: he leadeth me beside the still waters.—*Psalm* xxiii. 1, 3.	The Lamb . . . shall feed them, and shall lead them unto living fountains of water.—*Rev.* vii. 17.
37.	**37.**
Whom Jehovah loveth, he correcteth.—*Prov.* iii. 12.	As many as I love, I rebuke and chasten.—*Rev.* iii. 19.
38.	**38.**
God will render to them . . . eternal life.—*Rom.* ii. 5, 7.	Be thou faithful unto death, and I will give thee a crown of life.—*Rev.* ii. 10.
For he hath prepared (ἡτοίμασε) for them a city.—*Heb.* xi. 16.	I go to prepare (ἐτοιμάσαι) a place for you.—*John* xiv. 2.
39.	**39.**
[For all people will walk every one in the name of his god] and we will walk in the name of the Lord our God, (ἐν ὀνόματι Κυρίου Θεοῦ ἡμῶν) *LXX.*—*Micah* iv. 5.	And whatsoever ye do in word or deed, do all in the name of the Lord Jesus (ἐν ὀνόματι Κυρίου ᾿Ιησοῦ).—*Col.* iii. 17.
Let him trust in the name of the Lord, and stay upon his God.—*Isai.* l. 10.	And his name through faith in his name hath made this man strong.—*Acts* iii. 16.
Glorify ye....the name of the Lord God of Israel in the isles of the sea.—*Isai.* xxiv. 15.	That the name of our Lord Jesus Christ may be glorified in you.—*2 Thess.* i. 12.
The name of the Lord is a strong tower.—*Prov.* xviii. 10.	In his name shall the Gentiles trust.—*Matt.* xii. 21.
40.	**40.**
I will greatly rejoice in the Lord, my soul shall be joyful in my God: for he hath clothed me with the garments of salvation.—*Isai.* lxi. 10.	Jesus Christ: whom having not seen, ye love; in whom, though now ye see him not, yet believing, ye rejoice with joy unspeakable and full of glory: receiving the end of your faith, even the salvation of your souls.—*1 Pet.* i. 8, 9.
41.	**41.**
That God may be all in all (τὰ πάντα ἐν πᾶσιν).—*1 Cor.* xv. 28.	Christ, all and in all (τὰ πάντα καὶ ἐν πᾶσιν).—*Col.* iii. 11.
42.	**42.**
God and our Father: to whom be glory for ever and ever. Amen.—*Gal.* i. 4, 5.	Our Lord and Saviour, Jesus Christ. To him be glory both now and for ever. Amen.—*2 Pet.* iii. 18.

Let us ponder these passages with prayer. Here
Scripture asserts, that the Father is eternal, and the
Son eternal. Now One, who is from everlasting, must
needs be God. But there are not two Gods. Therefore the Son is one with God, and is God.

In like manner Scripture asserts that the Son,
equally with the Father, is the first and the last; is
omnipresent, immutable, almighty; is incomprehensible, absolutely holy, indefectible; is the Creator,
Preserver, and Governor of all things in heaven and
earth; is the Searcher of all hearts, the final Judge,
and the Awarder of everlasting life and death. Now
One, possessing such properties and fulfilling such
offices, must needs be God. But there are not two
Gods. Therefore the Son is one with God, and is God.

So, likewise, Scripture asserts, that unto the Son,
equally with the Father, his people are to cleave, in
him to abide, from him to draw their strength, and on
him to repose their hope and trust; that the Son,
equally with the Father, is the alone Saviour and
Redeemer of mankind; that looking up to the Son,
equally with the Father, sinners are pardoned and
souls are saved; that unto the supereminent Father,
and equally unto the supereminent Son, every knee
shall bow; that the Son, equally with the Father, is
the righteousness and strength and rock, the Shepherd
and the Master of his people; forgives sins, calms the
conscience, gives his holy Spirit, legislates for his
people on earth, and will receive them to his glory;
that the Son, equally with the Father, claims the supreme affiance of all, and is to those, who believe in him,
the Author of unspeakable joy and everlasting salvation. Now One, who is the object of such ultimate
confidence, homage, and delight, must needs be God.

52   THE TRINITY

But there are not two Gods. Therefore the Son is one with God, and is God.

Or, to put the same truth in another light, if you were asked to name the most marked relations, which Scripture represents the most high God as bearing towards his people, you would answer instinctively and without hesitation, those of Creator, Preserver, Redeemer, Saviour, Lord, Shepherd, King, Judge, and Father. And yet we read of Jesus Christ, as we have seen in the above passages, sustaining all these offices. Is he not our Creator, when "all things that are in heaven and that are in earth" were created by him? Is he not our Preserver, when "by him all things consist?" Is he not our Redeemer, seeing that "Christ hath redeemed us from the curse of the law, being made a curse for us?" Are not Saviour and Lord his distinctive names? Is he not emphaticaliy the Chief Shepherd (ὁ ἀρχιποιμήν)? Is he not the Lamb our King, when he is Lord of lords and King of kings? Is he not our Judge, when "we shall all stand before the judgment-seat of Christ?" And, lastly, does he not bear the relationship of Father to his people, when in them he sees his seed, the travail of his soul, and is satisfied; when he calls them children; and when he will present them at last before the throne, saying, "Behold I and the children which God hath given me?" Just as, if you took those passages only which refer to the Father under these characters, you might, without further search, have concluded that he alone, without the Son, bore these offices of love; so, likewise, if you were to take those Scriptures only which relate to the Son, you might have prematurely inferred, that Jesus Christ alone, without the Father, was the Creator, Preserver,

Col. i. 16, 17.

Gal. iii. 13.

1 Pet. v. 4.

Rev. xvii. 14.

Rom. xiv. 10.

Isai. liii. 10, 11.

John xxi. 5.

Heb. ii. 13.

Redeemer, Saviour, Lord, Shepherd, King, Judge, and Parent of his people.

These Scriptures are amply sufficient to bear the weight of this most solemn conclusion, and I might with blessed expectation ask—"Dost thou now believe in the Son of God?" But abounding and independent evidence remains.

(2) For the appearances of Jehovah to the Old Testament saints, taken in connection with the assertion to Moses, "Thou canst not see my face: for there shall no man see me, and live," and with the parallel ^{Ex. xxxiii. 20.} declaration of the New Testament, "No man (or no one, οὐδείς,) hath seen God at any time; the only begotten Son, which is in the bosom of the Father, he hath declared him," indicate that he, who thus mani- ^{John i. 18.} fested himself, was the Lord Jesus. It is true that in John i. 18, the assertion is general, *no one;* but in 1 Tim. vi. 16, "man" is expressed (ὃν εἶδεν οὐδεὶς ἄνθρωπος οὐδὲ ἰδεῖν δύναται), "whom no man hath seen, nor can see."

Now Jacob says, "I have seen God face to face, and my life is preserved," and this after wrestling all night ^{Gen. xxxii. 30.} long in tangible conflict with One now called a man, ^{Hosea xii. 3,4.} now the angel, now God, now the Lord God of hosts. The elders saw the God of Israel. Unto Moses, the ^{Ex. xxiv. 10.} Lord spake face to face, as a man speaketh with his ^{Ex. xxxiii. 11.} friend. Joshua conversed with the adorable captain of Jehovah's host. Manoah feared, saying, "We shall ^{Joshua v. 15, cf. Ex. iii. 5.} surely die, because we have seen God." Isaiah cried, ^{Judges xiii.22.} "Woe is me! for I am undone; . . . for mine eyes have seen the King, the Lord of hosts." Of the message ^{Isai. vi. 5.} then recorded, we are expressly told—"These things said Esaias, when he saw his (Christ's) glory, and spake of him." ^{John xii. 41.}

These are only selected passages. There are many others (compare Genesis xviii. 1, 2, with 17: Gen. xxxi. 11, with 13; Gen. xlviii. 15, with 16: Exod. iii. 2, with 4, 6: Exod. xiii. 21, with xiv. 19: Judges vi. 12, with 14, 22 with 23) in which the one who appears under the form of an angel or a man, is, in the immediate context, declared to be God, or Jehovah. Who, I ask, was this mysterious being? the Angel, or Sent One: he whom the Lord calls "*my presence;*" the visible similitude of Jehovah: an Angel of whom the Lord says, "Beware of him, and obey his voice, provoke him not; for he will not pardon your transgressions: for my name is in him?" This one could not be distinctively the Father, for no man hath seen him at any time, or can see him and live. But he who appeared is declared to be Jehovah and God. Are we not compelled to acknowledge that he was the Divine Word, the Son, the brightness of his Father's glory, the express image of his person? Therefore the Word is Jehovah God.

Ex. xxxiii. 14.
Num. xii. 8.

Ex. xxiii. 20
21.

(3) This is further established by the consideration that Scripture sanctions prayer to Christ, and commands the highest adoration and worship to be paid to him.

Respect being had to the argument of the preceding section, we may conclude that it was not distinctively God the Father, but God the Son with whom Abraham interceded for Sodom and Gomorrah. It was God the Son with whom Jacob wrestled in prayer, for we are told—"he had power with God: yea, he had power over the Angel, and prevailed," when he cried, "I will not let thee go, except thou bless me." It was God the Son, whose benediction he besought for his grand-children, when he prayed, "The God which

Gen. xviii. 23–
33.

Hosea xii. 3, 4.

fed me all my life long,. . . .the Angel which redeemed
me from all evil,˙ bless the lads." In all these in- ^{Gen. xlviii. 15,} _{16.}
stances, there is direct prayer to Christ.

Again, it was God the Son, called the Angel of Jehovah, whom Moses worshipped at the bush. It was
God the Son, who appeared as a man before whom
Joshua fell on his face and worshipped. It was God ^{Josh. v. 13, 14.}
the Son whose glory Gideon feared, and to whom he ^{Judg. vi. 24.} The Lord send
built the altar which records that living prayer, Jeho- ^{peace.}
vah-shalom. It was God the Son, the angel of Jeho-
vah, whose name was Wonderful, who rose in the
smoke of Manoah's sacrifice. It was God the Son, for ^{Judg. xiii. 17.} 20.
"upon the likeness of the throne was the likeness as
the appearance of a man above upon it," before whom ^{Ezek. i. 26.}
Ezekiel fell upon his face. In all these instances, we
have direct worship paid to Christ.

Further, we read expressly in the Gospels, that the
Lord Jesus was again and again worshipped, and we
never find that he refused this adoration. I cannot
consent for a moment to relinquish this word "worship" on the demand of some* Unitarian writers,
that it was only such reverent salutation, as was by
custom offered to those in authority. But at the same
time this demand requires that we carefully and can-
didly investigate the instances of its occurrence. No
one denies that the word translated worship (προσχυνέω) is often used in classical writers for humble and
prostrate salutation. But the great question remains,

---

* Thus Dr. Channing writes in reply to this argument, "It is
wonderful that this fallacy so often exposed should be still repeated. Jesus indeed received worship or homage, but this was
not as adoration to the infinite God: it was the homage which
according to the custom of the age, and of the Eastern world, was
paid to men invested with great authority, whether in civil or
religious concerns."—Quoted by Dr. Gordon.

what is its New Testament usage? I confess I was not prepared, when I began my search, for such preponderating proof of its almost universal application to Divine homage. The word occurs sixty times, and the noun formed from it (προσκυνητήτης)once. The references are given below.* From which we arrive at

---

* On the use of the word (προσκυνέω) in the New Testament:—

Worship offered to God.

Matt. iv. 10; \ Thou shalt worship the
Luke iv. 8, / Lord thy God.
John iv. 20—24, it occurs ten times including the noun—of the worship of the Father.
1 Cor. xiv. 25, he will worship God.
Rev. iv. 10, \ worship him that liveth
— v. 14, / for ever and ever.
— vii. 11, \
— xi. 16. } worshipped God.
— xiv. 7, worship him that made heaven.
— xv. 4, worship before thee, O Lord.
— xix. 4, worshipped God that sat on the throne.
— xix. 10, \
— xxii. 9. } worship God.

Idolatrous worship repudiated.

Matt. iv. 9, 10, \
Luke iv. 7, 8, } worship of Satan.
Acts vii. 43, worship of figures.
— x. 25, 26, human worship refused.
Rev. ix. 20, idolatry.
— xiii. 4 (twice), \
— xiii. 8, 12, 15, \
— xiv. 9, 11, \ worship of the
— xvi. 2, } dragon, the beast
— xix. 20, / or his image.
— xx. 4, /
— xix. 10, \ saintly or angelic wor-
— xxii. 8, 9, / ship refused.

Worship offered to Christ.

Matt. ii. 2, 8, 11, by the magi.
— viii. 2, by the leper.
— ix. 18, by the ruler.
— xiv. 33, by the disciples after the storm.
— xv. 25, by the woman of Tyre.
— xx. 20, by Salome.
— xxviii. 9, \ by the women and by
— xxviii. 17, } the disciples, after his resurrection.
Luke xxiv. 52, by the disciples as He ascended.
John ix. 38, by the man born blind.
Heb. i. 6, by all the angels.
[These are two instances of a distinct character:]
Mark v. 6, by the possessed.
— xv. 19, worship offered in mockery.

Worship used intransitively.

John xii. 20, Greeks came up to worship.
Acts viii. 27, of the eunuch.
— xxiv. 11, of Paul.
Heb. xi. 21, of Jacob.
Rev. xi. 1, worshippers in the temple.

[There remain two instances in which it is used of allowed salutation to man:]
Matt. xviii. 26, by the unmerciful servant.
Rev. iii. 9, I will make them to come and worship before thy feet.

this result, that there are twenty-two instances in which it is used of worship offered to God the Father, or absolutely to God; and five of Divine worsh;p used intransitively; fifteen instances (including two exceptional cases) of worship to Jesus Christ; seventeen of idolatrous worship condemned, and two only of allowed salutation to man. Of these last two, moreover, in one (Matt. xviii. 26,) the king to whom the worship is paid is in his royalty a type of God; and immediately after, when the story represents a like transaction between fellow-men, the word *worshipped* is exchanged for *besought.* We are, therefore, virtually reduced to one solitary instance; and taking the New Testament for our guide, it would be as unnatural to deny, that Divine worship is paid to Christ, as it would be just to accuse us of offering only human salutation to God, when we profess to *worship* him in his house, because we have lately addressed one of our civic magistrates as "the *worshipful* the mayor."

Matt.xviii. 29.

But the proportion of instances only presents a part of the evidence. When this same homage, described by the same word (προσχυνέω) was offered to a man or angel, where it could possibly be misunderstood, as by Cornelius to Peter, or by John to his prophetic guide, the action was immediately rebuked, and the worship straightway diverted from the creature to the Creator.

Acts x. 25, 26.
Rev. xix. 10;
xxii. 8, 9.

Nor is this all: it is not only, that Jesus was worshipped, but the affections and petitions, which accompanied that worship, manifest, if not always distinct recognition of his true Deity, at least, such humble dependence on his aid, as Divine aid, that if he were not God, he must needs have rectified so dangerous an approximation to idolatry. The leper not only worshipped him, but besought super-human assistance:

Matt. viii. 2. "Lord, if thou wilt, thou canst make me clean." The ruler not only worshipped him, but implored his Divine interference: "My daughter is even now dead: but come and lay thy hand upon her, and she shall Matt. ix. 18. live."* It was after he had manifested his God-like power in quelling the storm, that the disciples worshipped him, saying, "Of a truth thou art the Son of Matt. xiv. 33. God." He demanded the implicit confidence of the John ix. 35-38. man born blind, ere he received his worship. Natural love found utterance in that piercing prayer, when the woman of Tyre worshipped him, saying, "Lord, help Matt. xv. 2%. me." His resurrection power challenged and com-Matt. xxviii. 9. pelled the adoring worship of the Marys and the apostles; and the glory of the ascension warranted Luke xxiv. 52. the homage they paid on Olivet.

Nor are we confined to the word, *worship*. What was it but trustful prayer, when the disciples in the storm fulfilled the Psalmist's description of tempest-tossed Psa. cvii. 28. mariners, who "cry unto the Lord in their trouble," by betaking themselves to Jesus: "Lord, save us, we Matt. viii. 25. perish." What was it but prayer, when the two blind men implored a blessing no human power could be-Matt. ix. 27. stow, crying, "Thou Son of David, have mercy on us." The reader will easily multiply examples of these supplications from the gospel history.

Moreover, Jesus Christ inculcated prayer to himself. What petition could embrace a more glorious gift, than that he would persuade the woman of Samaria to offer? "Thou wouldst have asked of him, and he

---

* The distinction betwixt such petitions and the request to the apostles for assistance (as Acts ix. 38) is transparent; as Jesus in his own right, as the Messiah of God, wrought his mighty works; and they, utterly repudiating self-dependence (Acts iii. 12), wrought all in the name and by the power of Jesus Christ.

would have given thee living water,...springing up
into everlasting life." Again, he invites the weary John iv.10, 14
and heavy-laden to come to him for rest. How are Matt. xi. 28.
we to come, but by prayer? So he upbraids the Jews:
"Ye will not come to me, that ye might have life." John v. 40.
How were they to come, but by confiding prayer?
Yes, in confidence in a love, reliance on a power, dependence on a wisdom beyond that of our fellow-men
and beyond our own—this is the soul of prayer, this
is the essence of worship. But this trust he solicits
for himself. "Let not your heart be troubled: ye
believe in God, believe also in me." And so of praise. John xvi. 1.
You admit the Divine homage to the Father, of the
angelic song, "Glory to God in the highest:" You
must also admit the eucharistic tribute rendered,
though by humbler and human lips, when the multitudes cried, "Hosannah to the Son of David! Blessed
is he that cometh in the name of the Lord; Hosannah
in the highest." For, when the chief priests and Matt. xxi. 9.
scribes were sore displeased instead of rebuking this
giving of thanks, he says, "I tell you that, if these
should hold their peace, the stones would immediately
cry out. Have ye never read, Out of the mouth of Luke xix. 40.
babes and sucklings thou hast perfected praise?" Matt. xxi. 16.

Again, what was the dying act of the proto-martyr
Stephen, but the truest adoration of the Son of God?
Realize, I pray you, that scene. Stephen, full of the Acts vii.54-60.
Holy Ghost, looked up stedfastly into heaven and saw
the glory of God, and Jesus standing on the right
hand of God, and said, "Behold, I see the heavens
opened, and the Son of man standing on the right
hand of God." Then they cried out....and stoned
Stephen invoking,* and saying, "Lord Jesus, receive

---

* I need not remind the reader that the word *God* is not in the
Greek.

my spirit. And he kneeled down and cried with a loud voice, "Lord, lay not this sin to their charge." And when he had said this, he fell asleep. The Holy Ghost, who inspired David's devout affiance—"Into thine hand I commit my spirit: thou hast redeemed me, O Lord God of truth"—and who had dictated Solomon's declaration, "The spirit shall return unto God who gave it"—now, in the plentiude of his grace, prompted the dying martyr to pray not to God the Father alone, nor to the Father through Christ, but to pray to Christ, worshipping him with his latest breath as very and eternal God.

Again Paul addresses prayer to God the Father, and to the Lord Jesus Christ, without respect to order of names:—

Psa. xxxi. 5.

Eccle. xii. 7.

| Now God himself and our Father, and our Lord Jesus Christ direct our way unto you.—1 *Thess.* iii. 11. | Now our Lord Jesus Christ himself, and God, even our Father,....comfort your hearts.—2 *Thess.* ii. 16, 17. |

Here is express and direct supplication, so that we need not marvel that this was one distinctive name of Christian believers—"all that in every place call upon (ἐπικαλούμενος) the name of Jesus Christ our Lord."

The testimony from (ἐπικαλέομαι) here, and generally translated, "call upon," is most convincing, when compared with the Septuagint usage of the word: for it is the ordinary term for the sacred invocation of God; as, to take one example out of multitudes, "The Lord is nigh unto all them that call upon him, to all that call upon him in truth." It is employed in the New Testament for prayer to God the Father: "If ye call on the Father, etc." It describes such spiritual worship, that, whether offered to the Father or to the Son, salvation is indissolubly connected with it: "Whosoever shall call on the name of the Lord shall be

1 Cor. i. 2.

Psa. cxlv. 18.

1 Pet. i. 17.

saved.   And yet it is, without a shadow of a doubt, ^{Acts ii. 21.} applied to the invocation of the Lord Jesus—"all that call on thy name," "them which called on this name," ^{Acts ix. 14, 21.} and, (for the context compels us to interpret the following words of Christ,) "the same Lord over all, is rich unto all that call upon him."   Rom. x. 12.

When with an unbiassed mind you read, "Arise, and be baptized, and wash away thy sins, after calling on the name of the Lord," (ἐπικαλεσάμενος τὸ ὄνομα τοῦ ^{Acts xxii. 16.} Κυρίου), you make no question, that Divine worship is here intended. Or when you hear the practical command, "Follow after righteousness, faith, charity, peace, with them that call on the Lord out of a pure heart," (μετὰ τῶν ἐπικαλουμέ-νων τὸν Κύριον ἐκ καθαρᾶς ^{2 Tim. ii. 22.} καρδίας), no suspicion troubles your mind, that by these are not meant true spiritual worshippers.   Let us recur to the above-quoted description of the saints, "them that are sanctified in Christ Jesus, called saints, with all that in every place call upon the name of Jesus Christ our Lord, both theirs and ours." (σὺν ^{1 Cor. i. 2.} πᾶσι τοῖς ἐπικαλουμένοις τὸ ὄνομα τοῦ Κυρίου ἡμῶν ᾽Ιησοῦ Χριστοῦ ἐν παντὶ τόπῳ, αὐτῶν τε καὶ ἡμῶν). Is not this explicit? is not this Divine worship? are not these spiritual worshippers?   You must concede it.   And ALL SAINTS IN EVERY PLACE are thus worshipping Jesus Christ.   Consider this I pray you.   If you are appealed to by a friend in serious perplexity for counsel and succour, you give yourself up to his necessities. Your whole heart is engaged on his behalf.   But, if another man also in difficulty should chance to come at the same hour, you would find it hard to disengage your thoughts from the first case, and apply them to the second.   Now if a third suitor came for your deliberate judgment on a decision of the last importance, you would almost despair of keeping these varied interests disentangled and asunder. Suppose, however, ten or twenty anxious burdened suppliants were to besiege you at once, and all together to call upon you for immediate attention, for advice upon the spot, for aid at the moment, baffled and bewildered, you would retire alone and confess that such a demand was entirely beyond the powers of man. Now remember "ALL SAINTS IN EVERY PLACE ARE CALLING UPON THE NAME OF JESUS CHRIST." They are bringing before him matters of the most stupendous magnitude; they are pouring into his ear the deepest secrets of the human heart; they are supplicating grace for crises of the sorest need; they are confiding to his care the concerns of time and eternity. And what follows? He hears all. He comprehends all. He answers all. While receiving the adoration of the hosts of glory, he gathers up into his hand the woven tissue of the interests of his church militant here on earth. The worshippers are ten thousand times ten thousand and thousands of thousands. They are numbers without number. If a single cry of distress were disregarded, or a single note of praise unheard, that act of homage would be vain and futile, an offering to the idle air, an appeal to an incompetent Deity. But no prayer is lost. There is no confusion, no entanglement, no weariness, no intermission of regard. Himself has invited us to come, and ALL IN EVERY PLACE WHO CALL UPON HIS NAME are daily proving the truth of his Divine proclamation, "Come unto me, all ye that labour and are heavy laden, and I will give you rest."

Matt. xi. 28.

Before we pass on, let us ponder that declaration of Paul, with regard to his crucified Lord—"God hath highly exalted him, and given him a name which is above every name, that in the name of Jesus every

knee should bow, of *things* in heaven, and *things* in
earth, and *things* under the earth; and that every
tongue should confess that Jesus Christ is Lord, to the
glory of God the Father." Regard this fact as you Phil. ii. 9-11.
will, refine it as you may, spiritualize it to the utmost,
if Jesus were man only, it would prefigure the universal exaltation of a creature. The mighty suasion
of a creature's name, would bring every intelligent
being to his knees, from the highest archangel to the
feeblest saint: the name of a creature, would swell
the tide of celestial adoration, and tremble on the lips
of the contrite penitent; and the supremacy of a creature would overshadow heaven, and earth, and hell.
Could this tend to the glory of God the Father?
nay, verily. That name, which is above every name,
is Christ's, with emphatic propriety, "God, our Saviour."

The latest revelation of Scripture confirms this truth,
beyond contradiction. Is it Divine worship of the
Father, when Peter, having prayed the God of all
grace to perfect, stablish, strengthen, and settle his
people, closes his solemn prayer with the equally
solemn doxology, "To him be glory and dominion,
for ever and ever. Amen." You admit it, you call 1 Pet. v. 11.
it "adoration to the infinite God." Only be consistent. John, in Patmos, cries, "Unto him that loved
us, and washed us from our sins in his own blood, and
hath made us kings and priests unto God and his Father; to him be glory and dominion for ever and ever.
Amen." The words, both in Greek and English, are Rev. i. 5, 6.
identical; the adoration is the same; and the Beings
worshipped—the God of all grace, and the bleeding Compare also the doxology
Saviour—are One indivisible Jehovah. to Christ, 2 Pet. iii. 18.

And when the veil is drawn aside in the celestial
temple, what is, I pray you, the nature of their wor-

ship? O Spirit of the living God, engrave this transparent evidence on every doubting heart!

Rev. v. 8–14. "The four living creatures and four-and-twenty elders fell
down before the Lamb, having every one of them harps, and
golden vials full of odours, which are the prayers of saints.
And they sang a new song, saying, Thou art worthy to take the
book, and to open the seals thereof, for thou wast slain, and hast
redeemed us to God by thy blood, out of every kindred, and
tongue, and people, and nation; and hast made us unto our God
kings and priests: and we shall reign on the earth.

"And I beheld, and I heard the voice of many angels round
about the throne and the living creatures and the elders, and the
number of them was ten thousand times ten thousand and thousands of thousands; saying with a loud voice, Worthy is the
Lamb that was slain to receive power, and riches, and wisdom
and strength, and honour, and glory, and blessing.

"And every creature which is in heaven, and on the earth, and
under the earth, and such as are in the sea, and all that are in
them, heard I saying, Blessing, and honour, and glory, and
power, be unto him that sitteth upon the throne, and unto the
Lamb for ever and ever.

"And the four living creatures said Amen. And the four-
and-twenty elders fell down and worshipped him that liveth for
ever and ever."

This testimony is guarded on every side. You have
first, the redeemed adoring the Lamb only, with prostrate adoration. Then numbers without number of
the angels adore the Lamb likewise. Then the whole
universe, in similar adoration, blesses both the eternal
Father and the Lamb. And, lastly, there is the expressive echo of praise to the eternal Father alone.
You cannot say it is not the highest worship, for once
it is offered to the Eternal alone.* You cannot say it

---

* Or if, as is the most probable reading, you omit, with Tre-
gelles, in v. 14, the words, "Him that liveth for ever and ever,"
the worship is addressed absolutely to the Deity. It will scarcely

is offered to the Father alone, for once the Lamb is united with the Father. You cannot say it is offered to the Father only through the Son, for twice it is offered alone to the Lamb that was slain. It is the utmost homage heaven can pay. The spirits of the just made perfect have no higher tribute to give. The angels of light can offer no more exhaustive ascription of their devotion. No vision that you could have conceived, no language that you could have employed, could more distinctly authorize our rendering to Christ the highest and the deepest adoration, seraphic love, confiding trust, everlasting praise.

Is it possible that one question more lurks in any heart, why the Father only is here spoken of *on the throne*, and why the Lamb being God is not represented "in the seat of God?" Do the words of the Psalmist recur, "The Lord hath prepared his throne in the heavens." "God sitteth upon the throne of his holiness." "Thou satest in the throne judging right?" Let these Scriptures have their full weight. The possessor of the heavenly throne is God himself. The occupant of that throne is the Most High. Be it so. Then the last chapter of the Divine Revelation supplies the last proof of the one and equal supremacy of the Father and the Son, for there, repeated with solemn emphasis, we twice find the seat of the Eternal described, as THE THRONE OF GOD AND OF THE LAMB. _{Rev.xxii.1 & 3.}

Psa. ciii. 19; xlvii. 8; ix. 4.

I have dwelt the longer on this portion of my argument, for this is, of itself, sufficient to set the question at rest for ever, when we remember that Jesus Christ himself, gathering up the testimony of Scripture, says, "It is written, thou shalt worship ($\pi\rho\sigma\sigma\kappa\upsilon\nu\eta\sigma\epsilon\iota\varsigma$) the

---

be believed, that those who have refused to admit adoration as expressed by ($\pi\sigma\lambda\upsilon\mu\epsilon\rho\tilde{\omega}\varsigma$) when applied to Jesus Christ, have objected that here the self-same word is applied only to the Father.

Lord thy God, and him only shalt thou serve." But
we have seen that the highest worship and service on
earth, and in heaven, is rendered to the Son. Therefore, he is the Lord our God.

(4) Once more this truth is proved, by the conjunction of the name of the Lord Jesus with that of our
heavenly Father, in offices where the association of the
Creator with his creature, would confound the infinite
distinction betwixt God and man.

This evidence, though somewhat of a circumstantial
and incidental character, is from the exceeding solemnity of its use in the New Testament, peculiarly conclusive. The combination of the name of the Most
High with one subordinately employed in the evident
capacity of his servant, is of easy explanation: though
even this is rare in Scripture: but the conjunction of
the infinite God, with one co-ordinately engaged in
manifest equality of rank, is utterly inexplicable on
the Unitarian hypothesis. Examples will most readily
illustrate my meaning:—

"Go ye, and disciple all nations, baptizing them
into the name of the Father, and of the Son, and of
the Holy Ghost." Is it for a moment, conceivable,
that he who sees the end from the beginning, and
knew that this would be the standard formula of Christian baptism, would suffer that, in this most solemn
rite, the name of a creature with a derived being
should coalesce into his own name, which alone is Jehovah, the increate Father?

"He that loveth me shall be loved of my Father,
and I will love him: and will manifest myself unto
him. . . . . If a man love me he will keep my words:
and my Father will love him, and we will come to
him, and make our abode with him." The love of

the Father and of the Son is represented as an equal
privilege, the access of the Father and of his Son to
the soul of the obedient believer as a common access,
and the indwelling of the Father and of the Son as a
combined habitation. What created being could use
such language? It warrants the parallel declaration
of John's Epistle, "Truly our fellowship is with the
Father, and with his Son Jesus Christ," but it obliges ^{1 John i. 3.}
us, at the same time, to confess, that Jesus, in say-
ing God was his Father, made himself equal with
God.

"This is life eternal, that they might know thee the
only true God, and Jesus Christ whom thou hast sent." ^{John xvii. 3.}
Compare with this—"Grace and peace be multiplied
unto you through the knowledge of God, and of Jesus
our Lord." If Jesus Christ were only an angelic or hu- ^{2 Pet. i. 2.}
man prophet, revealing the Father, is it credible that
the intimate heart-knowledge of the expositor should
be put on the same level with the knowledge of God,
as equally essential to the life of the soul, and equally
indispensable for the sustenance of that life?

Again, I take up the Epistles. The prefaces are
most suggestive, whether you regard the embassy of
the writers, or the designation of the church addressed,
or the benediction implored.

As to the commission by virtue of which they acted,
you find almost every combination employed:—

"Paul, a servant of God, and an apostle of Jesus
Christ." ^{Tit. i. 1.}

"James, a servant of God and of the Lord Jesus
Christ." ^{James i. 1.}

"Peter, an apostle of Jesus Christ." ^{1 Pet. i. 1.}

"Simon Peter, a servant and an apostle of Jesus
Christ." ^{2 Pet. i. 1.}

"Jude, the servant of Jesus Christ." ^{Jude 1.}

"Paul, an apostle, . . by Jesus Christ, and God the Father, who raised him from the dead."

Would not this interchangeable variety, if Christ were man only, confuse every reverential distinction betwixt the Creator and the creature? Though here the difference betwixt the loftiest monarch and his lowliest subject sinks into nothing, can you imagine an earthly plenipotentiary sent forth, now styling himself "a servant of the emperor and an ambassador of the chancellor;" now "a servant of the emperor and of the chancellor;" now "an ambassador of the chancellor;" now "a servant and an ambassador of the chancellor;" now "the servant of the chancellor" now "an ambassador (sent) by the chancellor and by the emperor?" Who would not think that the imperial supremacy was greatly compromised by such language? And yet, there the distinction to be observed is only between two men of equal nature, though unequal rank. But no distinction is drawn in this celestial commission:—Is not then the original authority equal?

The designation of the churches addressed, is also perfectly unrestricted:—

"Unto the church of God which is at Corinth, to them that are sanctified in Christ Jesus."

"To the saints which are at Ephesus, and to the faithful in Christ Jesus."

"To all the saints in Christ Jesus which are at Philippi."

"Unto the church of the Thessalonians, which is in God the Father, and in the Lord Jesus Christ." Also

"The church . . . in God our Father, and the Lord Jesus Christ.

It is to these two last descriptions of the Thessalonian church I would especially direct your attention.

Was then their spiritual status equally indiscriminately consistent in the Father and the Son? Then to that church the Father and the Son were equally the Rock of their salvation.

And to complete the evidence, the benediction besought by the great apostle of the Gentiles is almost invariably in these words:*—

"Grace be unto you, and peace from God our Father, and the Lord Jesus Christ."

Why this mutual derivation of spiritual blessing from the Father and the Son? Surely, because equally in the Father and in the Son have we eternal life.

I might also adduce the prayers (quoted p. 60), where, without regard to precedence of names, blessings are implored from God the Father, and the Lord Jesus Christ himself, as co-equal in their power to grant the petition urged. 1 Thess.iii. 11.

2 Thess. ii. 16, 17.

But I hasten to that wondrous benediction which has dropped, as the gentle dew from heaven, upon the church of Christ for eighteen centuries—"The grace of the Lord Jesus Christ, and the love of God, and the communion of the Holy Ghost, be with you all. Amen." 2 Cor. xiii. 14.

Consider, I pray you, in the baptismal and in this benedictory formula, the meaning for which those who insist on the mere humanity of Jesus Christ con-

---

* I may mention, in passing, that there is a remarkable addition in the apostolic Epistles to Timothy and Titus. All the others that bear the name of Paul, begin with "Grace and peace;" these have a most gracious enlargement, "Grace, *mercy*, and peace." He who knew so well a minister's heart, interlined, as it were, his usual salutation-prayer, with *mercy*. How precious a word to ministers! And never more precious, than when treating of the awful mysteries of the faith.

tend.   The first, as expounded by them, would run
thus:—

*Baptizing them into the name of the Father, and of
an exalted man, and of a certain influence of the Father.*

The second would be thus interpreted:—

*The grace of a creature, and the love of the Creator, and
the communion of creative energy be with you all. Amen.*

Your reason and conscience alike, refuse to believe
that this inextricable confusion betwixt God and man,
between a person and an abstraction, is sanctioned by
Scripture.   And then in 2 Cor. xiii. 14, why this
notable change of the order observed in Matt. xxviii.
19, if not to show that "in this Trinity, none is afore
or after other, none is greater or less than another?"
These two verses, pondered and prayed over, seem to
me sufficient to decide the controversy for ever.

Creed of S.
Athanasius.

But if further testimony is needed, we have that of
every creature in heaven, and on the earth, and under
the earth, and such as are in the sea, and all that are
in them, who cry without intermission and without
pause, and therefore without the possibility of any
distinction, (as between the *dulia* and *latria* of the
Romanists,) being drawn in their adoration—"Blessing, and honour, and glory, and power, be unto him
that sitteth upon the throne, and unto the Lamb for
ever and ever."

Rev. v. 13.

Or, yet stronger proof if that were possible, we read
of the hundred forty and four thousand, not only harp-
ing with their harps and singing a new song which no
man could learn, but, as being themselves a living,
holy, acceptable sacrifice;—a sacrifice, unto whom?
unto the Father only? nay, they are "redeemed from
among men, the first-fruits unto God, and to the
Lamb."

Rev. xiv. 4.

And, finally of the glory of the heavenly Jerusalem,

CHAP. IV.

we read, "I saw no temple therein: for the Lord God Almighty and the Lamb are the temple of it. And the city had no need of the sun, neither of the moon, to shine in it: for the glory of God did lighten it, and the Lamb is the light thereof." Rev.xxi.22,23.

And when last we catch a glimpse of the throne of divine glory, whence flows the stream of crystal joy for ever, it is called, as we have seen, "the throne of God, and of the Lamb." Rev.xxii. 1-3.

Why (I press the question on your conscience) this co-equal and co-operating glory of the Lamb with the omnipotent God? Could you substitute any created man or angel for his excellent Name? Never. For he alone, in the unity of the Holy Ghost, is one with God, and is God. The Lord, of his infinite mercy, grant that I who write, and they who read these pages, may stand with that palm-bearing multitude of the redeemed, who have washed their robes, and made them white in the blood of Jesus, and who cry aloud ever more, "Salvation to our God which sitteth upon the throne, and unto the Lamb." Rev. vii. 10.

(5) It remains that we consider the explicit assertions that Jesus Christ is Jehovah and God.

These assertions are neither few nor obscure. But I would venture again to remind my readers, that the momentous inquiry in which we are engaged is no mere intellectual problem, to be grasped by the power of human reason, and to be solved by the skill of human analysis: for "no man can say that Jesus is the Lord, but by the Holy Ghost." And I would ask 1 Cor. xii.3. them to lift up their hearts with me, that the Spirit of truth may guide us into all truth, that he may glorify Jesus, and that he may take of the things of Christ, and show them unto us. John xvi. 13, 14.

"The title JEHOVAH is the grand, the peculiar, and the incommunicable name of God. It neither is applied to any created being throughout the Scriptures, nor can be applied in reason, for it imports the necessary, independent, and eternal existence of the Most High. Of the infinite, self-existent essence implied by this name, it is impossible for us to form a full and adequate idea; because we and all other creatures have but a finite derivative essence. Our sublimest notions of such uncircumscribed existence must fall infinitely more short of the truth, than the smallest animalcule or atom floating in the air, of the vast dimensions of universal nature. We could not even have conceived anything of the peculiarities which this name teaches us of the Almighty, if he had not been pleased to reveal himself under it, and to declare those distinguishing peculiarities to us."

Serle's Horae Solitariae.

Now we find certain prophetic declarations in the Old Testament regarding Jehovah fulfilled, as ruled by the New Testament, in Christ Jesus. This is, perhaps, the most conclusive evidence that could be adduced—an inspired interpretation of an inspired text —so that, if I may adopt the apostle's words, "by two immutable things, in which it is impossible for God to lie, we might have a strong consolation, who have fled for refuge to lay hold upon the hope set before us."

Heb. vi. 18.

The voice of him that crieth in the wilderness, Prepare ye the way of Jehovah, make straight in the desert a highway for our God.—*Isai.* xl. 3.	This is he that was spoken of by the prophet Esaias, saying, The voice of one crying in the wilderness, Prepare ye the way of the Lord.—*Matt.* iii. 3.

Now John Baptist's voice, without controversy, was heard in the wilderness, preparing the way for Christ. Therefore, Christ is Jehovah, our God.*

---

* So it results from a comparison of Luke i. 76, and Matt. xi. 10, that Jesus Christ is the Lord and the Highest. Cf. Jones, p. 4.

Sanctify Jehovah of hosts himself; and let him be your fear, and let him be your dread. And he shall be for a sanctuary; but for a stone of stumbling and for a rock of offence to both the houses of Israel.—*Isai.* viii. 13, 14.

Unto you therefore which believe he (Christ) is precious; but . . . a stone of stumbling, and a rock of offence, even to them which stumble at the word, being disobedient.—1 *Pet.* ii. 7, 8.

The stone of stumbling, as Isaiah affirms, is "Jehovah of hosts himself," but as Peter interprets it, (for he is referring to what is contained in the Scripture, ver. 6,) this stone is Christ. Therefore Christ is Jehovah of hosts himself.

And I (Jehovah, which stretcheth forth the heavens, etc., *see* ver. 1) will pour upon the house of David, and upon the inhabitants of Jerusalem, the Spirit of grace and of supplications: and they shall look upon me whom they have pierced.—*Zech.* xii. 10.

And again another Scripture saith, They shall look on him (Christ) whom they pierced.— *John* xix. 37.

The prophet declares the one who is pierced is Jehovah speaking of himself, but according to John's inspired interpretation, Christ crucified is here predicted. Therefore Christ is "Jehovah which stretcheth forth the heavens, and layeth the foundation of the earth, and formeth the spirit of man within him."

Mine eyes have seen the King, Jehovah of hosts.—*Isai.* vi. 5.

These things said Esaias, when he saw his glory and spake of him.—*John* xii. 41.

The message recorded determines the occasion to be the same. Therefore Jesus Christ, of whom the inspired apostle is speaking, is Jehovah of hosts, before whom the seraphim veiled their faces in lowliest adoration.

I (Jehovah) have sworn by myself. . . . . .that unto me every knee shall bow, every

We shall all stand before the judgment-seat of Christ. For it is written, As I live, saith the

tongue shall swear.—*Isai.* xlv. | Lord, every knee shall bow to
23. | me, and every tongue shall con-
                                  | fess to God.—*Rom.* xiv. 10, 11.

Paul incontrovertibly establishes his assertion, that we shall stand at the judgment-seat of Christ, by this solemn oath of Jehovah, recorded by Isaiah. Therefore, Christ is Jehovah, who says, (ver. 21,) "There is no God else beside me; a just God and a Saviour: there is none beside me."

When we remember the solemn protest of Him who calls himself the jealous God—"I am Jehovah: that Isai. xlii. 8. is my Name: and my glory will I not give to another:"—and when we reflect on the awful judgments denounced on those who render to the creature the supreme worship due to the Creator, the above comparison of Scripture with Scripture, wherein the Holy Ghost interprets, explains, and applies his own language, presents the most irrefragable proof that Jesus Christ is the Eternal, Increate, Alone, Jehovah of hosts, the Highest, the Lord our God.

And here may be the most convenient place to introduce a few remarks on the witness we derive from the word "Lord." No doubt it is often used by classical, and sometimes by the sacred writers, as a human appellation. But then the facts remain, that it is the word, equivalent to Adonai, which the Jews, through their reluctance to pronounce the awful name Jehovah, continually employed as its synonym; that it is the word by which Jehovah is uniformly translated by the Septuagint, even in Exodus vi. 3; and further, that standing by itself in the New Testament, it designates in multiplied passages the Infinite Father. We must look, therefore, broadly to its general use by Christ and his apostles. And what is the result? The word Κύριος occurs 737 times in the New Testament—of these, in 18 instances it is confessedly applied to man or men. In 54 instances it appears in the discourses and parables of Christ, where the master, described as Lord, represents or typifies the Father or himself: and in 665 cases, the vast remainder, it is applied indiscriminately to the Eternal Father or to the Son. Lists of the first two classes are given below.* Now in these eighteen instances (with scarcely an exception) there was not the remotest possibility of divine worship being intended to the person thus designated: indeed, in twelve of these cases, the word is in the plural. But what of those very numerous instances in which it is applied to Jesus Christ? Therein he is described as "Lord of all." Acts x. 36.

---

* Instances in which the word κύριος occurs in the discourses and parables of the Gospels, where the lord, master, or householder represents or typifies God the Father, or God the Son:—

Matthew vi. 24: x. 24, 25: xiii. 27: xviii. 25, 26, 27, 31, 32, 34; xx. 8: xxi. 30, 40: xxiv. 45, 46, 48, 50: xxv. 18—26, ten times.

Mark xii. 9: xiii. 35.

Luke x. 2: xii. 36—47, seven times: xiii. 8: xiv. 21, 22, 23: xvi. 3, 5, 8: xix. 16, 18, 20, 25: xv. 13, 15.

John xiii. 16: xv. 15, 20.

I was in some doubt whether to add to this list—

Matthew xxv. 11: Luke xiii. 25: but in these addresses the parable seems almost lost in the reality.

Instances in which the word κύριος is used of man—

Matt. xxvii. 63, by the Jews to Pilate.

Luke xix. 33, of the *owners* of the colt.

John xii. 21, by the Greeks to Philip.

Acts xvi. 16, 19, *masters* of the damsel.

— xvi. 30, by the jailer to Paul and Silas.

— xxv. 26, by Festus, of Augustus,

1 Cor. viii. 5, lords many.

Gal. iv. 1, of the heir.

Ephes. vi. 5, 9,
Col. iii. 22: iv. 1, } of masters.

1 Tim. vi. 15, [Lord] of lords.

1 Pet. iii. 6, by Sara, of Abraham.

Rev. vii. 14, by John to the elder.

— xvii. 14: xix. 16, [Lord] of lords.

Now it is trifling with this question to assert that the passages adduced in the *second column*, invalidate all the proof to be derived from the hundreds of passages in which Jesus Christ is called Lord, and as Lord is believed in, served and worshipped. The servant of a nobleman who addresses him as "my lord," does not confound his duty to his master and his God.

Acts ix. 17.

2 Cor. xii. 8, 9.

1 Cor. xv. 47.

2 Tim. iv. 8.

as the Lord, even Jesus, he appeared to Saul in vision: as the Lord, Paul besought him to remove his thorn in the flesh: he is declared to be the second man, the Lord from heaven: and as the Lord, the righteous Judge, he will give a crown of righteousness to all them that love his appearing. Now to one thus described as Lord, seeing that the name is applied to the Father and the Son indiscriminately, so that, in many places, the difficulty is very great of knowing whether the Eternal Father or the Lord Jesus Christ be intended, the risk of ascribing divine worship would be imminent indeed. The collation of two passages from the Old, with two passages from the New Testament, seems to clinch the argument:—

Hear, O Israel: the LORD our God is one LORD (Κύριος ὁ Θεὸς ἡμῶν, Κύριος εἶς ἐστι—*LXX*—*Deut.* vi. 4.	There is one Lord (εἷς Κύριος) *Eph.* iv. 5.
And the LORD shall be king over all the earth. In that day shall there be one Lord, and his name One. (Κύριος εἶς καὶτὸ ὄνομα αὐτοῦ ἓν—*LXX*—*Zech.* xiv. 9.	To us......there is......one Lord (εἷς Κύριος) Jesus Christ, by whom are all things, and we by him.—1 *Cor.* viii. 6.

Here the apostle uses the very words to which the Jews clung with such tenacity as establishing the fundamental truth of the Unity of God; and adopting the very words of the common version, the Septuagint, applies them to Jesus Christ. There appears, therefore, in this name of Christ, *as used in the New Testament,* explicit declaration that he is the Eternal Jehovah.

As a link of connection between the testimony of the Old and New Testament to the person of the Messiah, I would now entreat the reader's calm and prayerful consideration of the first two chapters of the Epistle to the Hebrews. The writer is proving the pre-eminence of Christ over all other prophets, and the essential difference betwixt his and the angelic nature. If exorbitant views of his Divine dignity had crept into the church, here, at least, we should look for the correction of error, and for definition of the truth. And how then is he described?

"God, who at sundry times and in divers manners spake in time past unto the fathers by the prophets, hath in these last days spoken unto us by his Son, whom he hath appointed heir of all things, by whom also he made the worlds; *Or "in many fragments." πολυμερῶς little by little, Cf. 1 Cor. xiii.9, ἐκ μέρους*

"Who being the brightness of his glory, and the express image of his person (ὑποστάσεως), and upholding all things by the word of his power, when he had by himself purged our sins, sat down on the right hand of the Majesty on high; being made so much better than the angels, as he hath by inheritance obtained a more excellent name than they.

"For unto which of the angels said he at any time, Thou art my Son, this day have I begotten thee? And again, I will be to him a Father, and he shall be to me a Son. And again, when he bringeth in the first-begotten into the world, he saith, And let all the angels of God worship him.

"And of the angels he saith, Who maketh his angels spirits, and his ministers a flame of fire.

"But unto the Son he saith, Thy throne, O God, is for ever and ever: a sceptre of righteousness is the sceptre of thy kingdom: Thou hast loved righteousness, and hated iniquity; therefore God, even thy God, hath anointed thee with the oil of gladness above thy fellows. And Thou, Lord, in the beginning hast laid the foundation of the earth; and the heavens are the works of thine hands: they shall perish: but thou remainest; and they all shall wax old as doth a garment; and as a vesture shalt thou fold them up, and they shall be changed: but thou art the same, and thy years shall not fail."*

Heb. i. 1–12.

I would only here again remind you, that we have a Divine interpretation of the Divine Scriptures. What-

---

* The most severe criticism has not really brought one sustained objection against the received version.

ever be your preconceived view of these verses, the apostle, writing as he was moved by the Holy Ghost, adduces them as *proof texts* of the glory of Christ. In the following chapter, we find this wonderful Saviour Heb. ii. 9, 10. made a little lower than the angels, for the suffering of death, perfected through suffering, taking part of Heb. ii. 14, 17, 18. flesh and blood, in all things made like unto his brethren, having suffered, being tempted: but in these verses I have quoted, how transcendent his Majesty! The goodly fellowship of the prophets were his forerunners. The innumerable company of angels are his worshippers. He is seated on the everlasting throne. He is the only-begotten Son of the Father, He is addressed as God. He is adored as the immutable, immortal Jehovah. I feel any attempt to enforce this evidence may mar its impressive grandeur, and I can only pray that the word of God may here be quick and powerful, and sharper than any two-edged sword, in the hand of the Almighty Spirit of God.

I might well close this part of my argument here. Scripture declares that our God, whose name alone is Jehovah, is One Jehovah, and is jealous of his own attributes and of our confidence. In a word, we rest on God. At the same time, Scripture declares that all these Divine attributes belong to Jesus Christ, who claims equal adoration and equal trust, as being himself Jehovah, our God and Saviour. Our faith centres on Jesus Christ. Christ is all, and in all, to the Christian. In a word, we rest on Christ. Here is our Rock, *inexpugnabile saxum.* You cannot add to its security, for it is impregnable. You cannot increase its stability, for it is immovable. You cannot make absolute certainty more certain. Nevertheless, many express assertions remain. And if I may return to

my former illustration from trigonometry, in the solu-
tion of a triangle, if a side be measured and two angles
be observed, nothing can add to the perfect certainty
with which a mathematician tells you the number of
degrees in the third angle, and the length of the re-
maining sides. Nothing would increase his assurance.
His conclusion is demonstrably true. Still if an independent observer could tell you the measurement of
those parts which were the object of algebraic investigation, the fact of their precise coincidence, which of
course and of necessity appears, is a further proof with
what security you may always rest on the results of
mathematical science. I would, then, draw into a
brief compass some few of these positive declarations.
They state expressly what other Scriptures prove de-
monstratively.

Let us then humbly weigh that passage, against John i. 1–14.
which sceptical criticism has directed its fiercest at-
tacks, but from which they have all recoiled, and
which stands impregnable as ever, a rock foundation
for the faith of the humble believer.

"In the beginning was the Word, and the Word was with
God, and the Word was God. The same was in the beginning
with God. All things were made by him; and without him was
not any thing made that was made. In him was life: and the
life was the light of men. And the light shineth in darkness;
and the darkness comprehended it not. There was a man sent
from God, whose name was John. The same came for a witness, to bear witness of the Light, that all men through him
might believe. He was not that light, but was sent to bear
witness of that light. That was the true light, which lighteth
every man that cometh into the world. He was in the world,
and the world was made by him, and the world knew him not.
He came unto his own, and his own received him not. But as
many as received him, to them he gave power to become the
sons of God, even to them that believe on his name; which

were born, not of blood, nor of the will of the flesh, nor of the will of man, but of God. And the Word was made flesh, and dwelt among us, (and we beheld his glory, the glory as of the only begotten of the Father,) full of grace and truth. . . . . No man hath seen God at any time: the only begotten Son which is ver. 18. in the bosom of the Father, he hath declared him."*

Hence we learn that the Word was co-eternal with God in the beginning, was God, was the Maker of all things, was the Fountain of life and light to men, dwelt incarnate amongst us, and thus himself, the only-begotten Son, declared the Invisible Father. That by the Word is designed the Lord Jesus Christ is transparent. If anything however could add to our assurance of this, it would be the fact of Philo, a Jew of Alexandria, contemporary with Christ, but manifestly ignorant of his history, describing THE DIVINE WORD, as the Son of God, the First Begotten, the Image of God, the Angel, a second God, the instrument of Deity in the creation, the High Priest and Mediator, per-fectly sinless himself, and the fountain of virtue to men: and of John adopting this self-same name, THE WORD, as one indicative of the Messiah, and un-

---

*I earnestly recommend the reader to weigh Dr. Pye Smith's lucid exposition of this passage, and pray that the question he puts into the lips of the sincere Unitarian may be applied with Divine power.—"Am I not inwardly sensible that, in my attempts to frame an interpretation of this paragraph, which may bear at all the semblance of consistency, I am rowing against the stream, I am putting language to the torture; I am affixing significations to words and phrases, which all my efforts can scarcely keep me from exclaiming could never have been in the contemplation to the original writer? Have I not then awakening reasons for the suspicion that I have not framed my opinions with that close and faithful investigation, which the solemn greatness of the case re-quires? Am I not bound to review the whole subject in the sight of the all-seeing God, and under the sense of my accountableness to him as the author and revealer of truth?"

derstood by those who should read his Gospel. But Scripture is its own best interpreter. And this same apostle, writing in after years of the advent of Christ says, "He was clothed with a vesture dipped in blood; and his name is called THE WORD OF GOD." Christ ^{Rev. xix. 13.} then is the Word, Christ is the Creator, Christ is God. This introduction to his Gospel was, I doubt not, constructed by the inspired apostle to be a bulwark against every doubt, and accordingly, for near two thousand years,

> "as a tower of strength,
> Which stood four-square to every wind that blew,"

it has kept the hearts of innumerable believers in perfect peace.

There is another passage I cannot pass over, though space forbids me to enter into it fully.

"But Jesus answered them, My Father worketh hitherto, and I work. Therefore the Jews sought the more to kill him, because he not only had broken the sabbath, but said also that God was his Father, making himself equal with God. Then answered Jesus, and said unto them, Verily, verily, I say unto you, The Son can do nothing of himself, but what he seeth the Father do: for what things soever he doeth, these also doeth the Son likewise. For the Father loveth the Son, and showeth him all things that himself doeth: and he will show him greater works than these, that ye may marvel. For as the Father raiseth up the dead, and quickeneth them; even so the Son quickeneth whom he will. For the Father judgeth no man but hath committed all judgment unto the Son: that all men should honour the Son, even as they honour the Father. He that honoureth not the Son honoureth not the Father which hath sent him. Verily, verily, I say unto you, He that heareth my word, and believeth on him that sent me, hath everlasting life, and shall not come into condemnation; but is passed from death unto life. Verily, verily, I say unto you, The hour is coming, and now is, when the dead shall hear the voice of the

Son of God: and they that hear shall live. For as the Father hath life in himself; so hath he given to the Son to have life in himself; and hath given him authority to execute judgment also, because he is the Son of man. Marvel not at this: for the hour is coming, in which all that are in the graves shall hear his voice, and shall come forth: they that have done good, unto the resurrection of life; and they that have done evil, unto the resurrection of damnation." John v. 17—29.

The Jews accused our Lord of making himself equal with God, because he said God was his Father. What is his reply? Instead of protesting against their construction of his words, which if only a man, he would have done with indignation and abhorrence, he proceeded, while acknowledging the subordinatoin of his mission as man, to set forth the original and essential supremacy of his person as God. For if the Son doeth all things what things soever the Father doeth: if the Son quickeneth whom he will: if the dead shall hear his voice and live: if he executes judgment on the universe; if all men must honour the Son, even as they honour the Father: then is he equally Almighty: equally the communicative fountain of life: equally God who alone can raise the dead: equally the Omniscient who alone can judge an assembled world: and equally the centre of universal homage and adoration.

ver. 19.
ver. 21.
ver. 27.

ver. 23.

I proceed to the utterance of Thomas, when the permitted touch of his risen Saviour scattered the dark clouds of unbelief—"My Lord and my God!" I know that it has been alleged that this was an exclamation of surprise, addressed to God the Father; but I can hardly believe any earnest seeker after truth can thus be baffled. No one who knows the language of the heart, can here misinterpret it. The apostle had given up all for Jesus Christ: his Master had been

John xx. 28.

seized, and crucified, and buried: and Thomas's faith
was sorely tried. But now his Lord stood before him—
he could doubt no more; and "he answered and said"
(not without reason is the word "answered" here
inserted—the words were addressed as an answer to
One who stood his proven Saviour before him:—it was
the deep response of the heart of Thomas to Christ,)
"he answered and said, My Lord and my God!"

I append other passages with a few brief remarks
of the most learned and impartial critics:—

Rom. ix. 5,—"Of whom as concerning the flesh
Christ came, who is over all, God blessed for ever."

"Every Greek scholar must admit, that the fair
and just construction of the sentence is that which is
generally received."—P. Smith, vol. ii, p. 683.

Col. ii. 9,—"for in him dwelleth all the fulness of
the Godhead bodily."

"*The Godhead*, i. e., Deity, the essential being of
God—*bodily*, i. e., manifested corporeally in his present
glorified body. Before his incarnation, it dwelt in
him as the λόγος ἄσαρκος, but not σωματικῶς, as now
that he is the λόγος ἔνσαρκος.—Alford.

Ephes. v. 5,—"The kingdom of [him who is] Christ
and God (ἐν τῇ βασιλείᾳ τοῦ Χριστοῦ καὶ Θεοῦ)."

"Not only the principle of the rule and the invari-
able practice of the New Testament with respect to
Θεός, and all other attributives, compel us to acquiesce
in the identity of Χριστοῦ καὶ Θεοῦ, but the same truth
is evinced by the examination of the Greek fathers."
. . . Middleton, quoted by P. Smith, who says, "If
this text had no relation to any controversy, and were
judged of solely by the common law of Greek construction, no person would ever have disputed the propriety,
or rather necessity, of considering the two concluding
nouns as referring to one and the same object."

Titus ii. 13,—"the glorious appearing of our great God and Saviour, Jesus Christ.

Cf. Scholefield's note in his "Hints." Middleton says, "If here the sacred writer did not mean to *identify* the great God and the Saviour, he expressed himself in a manner which [could not but] mislead his readers."—Quoted by P. Smith.

2 Pet. i. 1,—"the righteousness of our God and Saviour, Jesus Christ (ἐν δικαιοσύνῃ τοῦ Θεοῦ ἡμῶν καὶ σωτῆρος 'Ιησοῦ Χριστοῦ): for construction compare the expression a little below,—(ver. 11,) "the everlasting kingdom of our Lord and Saviour Jesus Christ (τὴν αἰώνιον βασιλείαν τοῦ Κυρίου ἡμῶνκαὶ σωτῆρος 'Ιησοῦ Χριστοῦ)."*

And, lastly, 1 John v. 20,—"We are in him that is true, in his Son Jesus Christ. This (person) is the true God, and eternal life."

"The circumstance which, in my mind, places the matter beyond dispute is, that the same person is here most evidently spoken of as 'the true God and ETERNAL LIFE.' It will be granted that a writer is the best interpreter of his own phraseology. Observe, then, the expression which he uses in the beginning of the Epistle. 'The life was manifested and we have seen it, and show unto you that ETERNAL LIFE, which was with the Father, and was manifested unto us.' In these words it is admitted that the eternal life is a title given to Jesus Christ. Compare, then, the two passages. Is not the conclusion of the Epistle a

1 John i. 2.

---

* If the Unitarians insist that both the Father and the Son are intended in these three passages, granting for a moment this were possible, then as an *argumentum ad seipsos,* all the force of the previous section (4) applies, and we find the conjunction of the names God and Christ, where such association would confound the distinction betwixt the Creator and his creature.

clear explanation of its beginning?"—Wardlaw's Discourses, p. 59.

I would only ask you to compare with this, the confession of the prophet, "Jehovah is the true God. He is the living God." And here we have another ^{Jer. x. 10.} invincible argument that Jesus Christ is Jehovah, very and eternal God.

This treatise does not profess to enter deeply into a critical examination of the text of the New Testament; but it may be a satisfaction to those whose minds have been disturbed by rash assertions of the uncertainty of manuscripts and versions, to know, that not one of the texts, here relied on, is set aside by that learned and eminent man, Dr. Grisbach.* To him Unitarians constantly appeal. Of him Dr. P. Smith writes: "No man ever devoted, through a long life, such a persevering assiduity of labour to the critical study of the New Testament, and no man has ever so completely united the confidence of all denominations of Christians in the sagacity, judgment, and integrity of his critical decisions." There are indeed *three* texts often contended for, which the authority of this distinguished professor precludes my bringing forward as evidence: 1 John v. 7, he believes to be an interpolation; in Acts xx. 28, he prefers κυρίου to Θεοῦ; and in 1 Timothy iii. 16, he would substitute ὅς for .Θεός). But to these

---

* On the doctrine before us, Griesbach says: "So numerous and clear are the arguments and testimonies of Scriptures in favour of the true Deity of Christ, that I can hardly imagine how, upon the admission of the Divine authority of Scripture, and with regard to fair rules of interpretation, this doctrine can by any man be called in doubt. Especially the passage, John i. 1—3, is so clear, and so superior to all exception, that by no daring efforts of either commentators or critics can it be overturned, or be snatched out of the hands of the defenders of the truth."—Quoted by P. Smith, vol. ii. p. 540.

three texts, that we may not be drawn into needless disputations, I have simply forborne to refer. The argument does not demand them. It is incontrovertible without them. And therefore the inquirer may be certified on the one hand, that if he rejected the positive assertions that Christ is God, the great God our Saviour, in whom dwelleth all the fulness of the Godhead bodily, he would be violating those rules of sound common sense which he must apply, to interpret every other classical work; and on the other hand, he may be assured, that in resting on these declarations he is, so far as the most calm and learned scholars can assure him, relying on the very exact meaning of the words intended by those who wrote under the inspiration of the Holy Ghost.

And here, I would pause, and pray the reader to review the impressive strength of that evidence which the word of God has afforded.

Let us remember how earnestly Scripture detaches our ultimate confidence from any creature, and exclusively claims it for the one Infinite Creator: how vivid is the contrast drawn betwixt man and God: how direct are the prohibitions against trusting in man, how express the precepts to rest on God: and moreover how awful is the holy jealousy of the Most High, if any one usurp the incommunicable glories of his name, or intrude upon the claims of his supremacy: so that the first great lesson of spiritual education may be summed up in the words—"Blessed is the man that trusteth in the Lord, and whose hope the Lord is."

Jer. xvii. 7.

Further let us remember, how confessedly Scripture requires us to repose our ultimate confidence in the Lord Jesus Christ: setting him before us, as possessed of all those incommunicable attributes of Godhead; as our Creator, Preserver, and final Judge; as the

hope of fallen man, to whom the eye of every believer
was directed by prophecy before his first advent; and
as the great object of religious trust, a trust claimed
by himself when he came into the world, conceded by
his followers, and commanded by his inspired apostles:
so that the second great lesson of spiritual education
may be summed up in these words—"Whosoever believeth in the Son of man shall not perish, but have
eternal life." John iii. 15.

Further let us remember, that comparing spiritual
things with spiritual, not only does Scripture ascribe
to Christ all the attributes of essential Deity, and thus,
seeing there is one God and none else, establish the
unity and equality of the Son with the Father; but
moreover represents the Son as fulfilling towards us
all those offices of infinite greatness and goodness
which God only can sustain: that the appearances of
God Jehovah to the Old Testament saints, combined
with the declaration, "No man hath seen God at any
time," are utterly inexplicable on any other hypothesis,
and are absolutely decisive when the New Testament
assures us, it was the glory of the Lord Jesus they saw:
that the direct and Divine worship rendered to and
received by Christ, in earth and heaven, compels us to
acknowledge he is the Lord our God: that the name
of Jesus Christ is united with that of our heavenly
Father in offices, where the coalition of the Creator
with his creature would blend and confuse the infinite
distinction betwixt God and man: that, whereas the
most sensitive jealousy appears, throughout Scripture,
of any created being usurping the name of the supreme
Creator, inspired interpretations of inspired texts assure us that Jesus Christ is the Eternal, Jehovah of
hosts, the Lord our God: that as Lord, the one Lord,
he requires obedience and is obeyed, claims trust and

is trusted, demands adoration, and is adored· and that, finally, he is addressed as God and Lord; that he, the Word, is declared to be God, to be with God in the beginning, to be the Creator of all; that he claims equal honour; that he is over all God blessed for ever; that his righteousness is the righteousness, and his future advent the appearance of our great God and Saviour Jesus Christ; and that of him John declares, "this is the true God and eternal life."

Let us ponder these things, and reflect how cumulative is this evidence. I earnestly pray that the Divine Spirit may present it with irresistible power to every conscience. If, after weighing the solemn declarations of Jehovah, guarding his own inalienable glories, we had found the essential attributes of Deity assigned in Scripture to Jesus Christ, this would have been an unanswerable argument. If, after considering our miserable condition as lost sinners, we had found that, in the matter of eternal salvation, our hopes are there directed to Jesus as our Saviour, this would have been conclusive evidence, when we remember, "I am God, and beside me there is no Saviour." If, leaving this line of proof, we review the appearances of the Lord to the Old Testament saints, this would have been a new and interesting series of demonstrations, which would lead us to the same result. If again, quitting this, we carefully ponder the Divine worship offered to him, and accepted by him, this is decisive, when we remember, "Thou shalt worship the Lord thy God, and him only shalt thou serve." If, pursuing another path of investigation, we study those Scriptures where, in offices of the highest solemnity, the name of Jesus Christ is so united with that of our heavenly Father, that to accept this as the conjunction of the Creator with his creature would confound all

distinction betwixt God and man, we are again led
irresistibly to the conclusion, that the Godhead of the
Father and of the Son is one, the glory equal, and
the majesty co-eternal. If once more we see how
prophecies regarding God Jehovah are claimed by the
New Testament as being fulfilled in Jesus Christ, here
is inspired testimony to the supreme Deity of the
Messiah. And finally, when we find the awful names
of God, and Saviour, and Redeemer, and Lord, ascribed
to him again and again, in a subject where misdirected
faith were idolatry and death, this again is explicit
assertion and transparent proof. I say, the evidence
is cumulative. It is not a long elaborate catena, the
strength of which is the strength of its weakest link.
If the reader thinks any text is inapplicable, let him
dismiss it. This proof rests on hundreds of texts.
The whole drift of Scripture, from Genesis to Revelation, establishes it. It is interwoven with the very
texture of the sacred writings. The lines of argument
are distinct and independent; and yet, when presented
in their collective strength, they are so mutually cor-
roborative, that it seems as if we heard the voice again
from heaven, saying, "This is my beloved Son, hear
ye him:" and when we humbly ask, "Who is he,
Lord, that I might believe in him?" and bend a reverential ear to catch the import of the answer, it is
this, "Unto you is born a Saviour, which is Christ the
Lord, Emmanuel, Wonderful, Counsellor, the mighty
God, the Father of eternity, the Prince of Peace."

But cordially to embrace this needs, I know, the convincing power of the Holy Ghost. I feel my helpless-
ness. I give myself to prayer. The altar is built as
once on Carmel, the trench is made, the wood is piled,
the sacrifice disposed in order. But it needs the fire
from heaven. "Hear me, O Lord, hear me: glorify

Gal. i. 16.

John vi. 44.

thy Son that thy Son may also glorify thee. Reveal thy Son to those who seek thee. Draw them unto him. Thou commandedst the light to shine out of darkness: shine in their hearts, shine in my heart, to give the light of the knowledge of the glory of God in the face

2 Cor. iv. 6.

of Jesus Christ."

Bear with me, my friends, for giving utterance to prayers, which have been long pleaded at the throne of grace. They have not been offered in vain. And when the fire of the Lord falls on any heart, it shall consume the sacrifice, and the wood, and the stones, and the dust; and the deep response of that believing soul shall be, "My Redeemer, thou art the Lord—my Saviour, thou art God."

CHAPTER V

CHAP. V.

I PROCEED, therefore, to my fourth proposition:— *That Scripture, in the Old and the New Testament alike, presents to us the incarnation and the mission of the Saviour, as the extremity of condescension in Jehovah, that thereby he might exalt us to everlasting life.*

(1) The Scriptures already cited prove beyond contradiction, the co-equal, co-essential, co-eternal Deity of the Son. And here we have attained that vantage ground from which, I am persuaded, we may most safely with the adoring angels stoop down and look into the humiliation and the humanity of Jesus

1 Pet. i. 12.

Christ.

Let us only follow the pathway along which Scripture does, as it were, lead us by the hand. Let us acknowledge the infinite perfections of him who is the alone Supreme Jehovah. Let us confess the infinite

demerit of rebellion against him. Let us admit that
he has opened to us in his word a way of access, whereby we, the sinful and the sunken, may be brought
nigh to him, the absolutely Holy and Good One, who
is "of purer eyes than to behold evil, and cannot look
on iniquity." Let us remember that this reconcile- Hab. . 13.
ment is spoken of as a salvation, to accomplish which
Omnipotence travels in the greatness of its strength, Isai. lxiii. 1.
and which Omniscience declares to have been a mystery
hidden in God from the beginning of the world: and Eph. iii. 9.
that to fulfil this work we find a wondrous mission revealed, in which the Lord God and his Spirit send
forth, and the Eternal I AM is the sent One. Let us Isai. xlviii. 16.
then on the sure testimony of Scripture acknowledge
that all the attributes, the honours, and the rights of
Jehovah are ascribed to this Sent One, whose name is
called Jesus, for he shall save his people from their Matt. i. 21.
sins; who claims himself equality with God as his
only-begotten Son; and who is associated with God in
every supreme office of Deity. And lastly, let us accept
the simple fact, as recorded in the Bible, of Christ's
descent from above, that he, the Word, who in the
beginning was with God and was God, was made flesh John i. 1, 14.
and dwelt among us; that he came down from heaven; John iii. 13.
that he proceeded forth and came from God, forsaking John viii. 42.
the glory which he had with the Father before the
world was; that being originally (ὑπάρχων) in the John xvii. 5.
form of God, he emptied himself, and took upon him
the form of a servant, and was made in the likeness of Phil. ii. 6, 7.
men: that by him the universal Creator—by him in-
carnate and crucified—it pleased the Godhead to reconcile all things unto himself: that he being the Col. i. 19, 20.
brightness of his Father's glory and the express image
of his person, in the bringing many sons of God to
glory, forasmuch as the children were partakers of

flesh and blood, also himself likewise partook of the
same, that through death he might destroy him that
had the power of death, that is, the devil, and deliver
them who through fear of death were all their life
Heb. i. 3; ii.
10, 14, 15. subject to bondage.

Now our whole souls are filled with one thought—
the condescension of God. Now we shall not be
stumbled at passages which speak of the exceeding
humiliation to which he stooped. As we assign no
limit to the height of his glory, we shall assign none
to the depths of his grace. Yea, so far from taking
offence at the inferiority of the position which he assumed, the very lowliness of his incarnation and the
very degradation of the death he died, will kindle in
us a brighter and more burning gratitude, when we
remember that though rich it was for our sakes he
2 Cor. viii. 9. became poor; and that for us, his wayward and wan-
dering sheep, the chief Shepherd offered up himself as
the Lamb of God, laying down his life of his own accord, and taking it up again to die no more.

(2) Perhaps to some minds it might have seemed
more congruous with the Divine Majesty, supposing it
needful for our salvation that God should humble himself at all, that the descent should have been less steep,
and the humiliation less lowly. They would have
chosen not some little insignificant planet like earth
as the scene of his self-abnegation, but some central
orb of metropolitan grandeur, and would have gathered
the whole intelligent creation as spectators around the
splendid arena. They would fain have had him assume
not the body of our abasement, but haply an angelic
nature, wherein, as some seraph of surpassing brightness, he should have wrought deeds of miraculous
beneficence. And chiefly, they would have shunned for
him the ignominy of the cross, and have selected what

they deemed some more glorious method of self-sacrifice, whereby he should have paid the price of our redemption. This they would have called a salvation worthy God. But surely, as the heavens are higher than the earth, so are the way of Jehovah higher than our ways and his thoughts than our thoughts. His ^{Isai. iv. 9-54-9} work is perfect. Let us remember that whatever of material and physical glory we add to the mission of Christ, beyond what is needful for the evidence of that mission, we subtract from its moral and spiritual glory. Between the unapproachable splendors of the Godhead, and the various forms of created intelligence there is a distance absolutely immeasurable. For the increate Jehovah to have assumed the nature of the highest archangel would have been an infinite descent. Let us thus far confide with childlike confidence, that herein was manifested omniscient love, when God chose the world—this little world of ours—to be the theatre of the mighty conflict, and sent his only-begotten Son in the likeness of sinful flesh to suffer death upon the cross, and to be the propitiation for our sins. Rom. viii. 3. 1 John iv. 9, 10.

"The Word was made flesh, and dwelt among us." There is a majestic condescension in these few words that nothing can equal. He was made man. "By himself, by his friends and disciples, by his enemies and persecutors, Jesus Christ was spoken of, as a proper human beling. His childhood was adorned with filial affection, and the discharge of filial duty. His intel-^{Luke ii. 40-52.} lectual powers, like those of other children, were progressive. In his earliest years, he embraced with eagerness the means of improvement. He had large experience of human suffering. His lot was one of severe labour, poverty, weariness, hunger, and thirst. He affected no austerity of manners, nor did he enjoin it upon his followers. While he mingled in the common sociability and the innocent festivities of life, he sustained a weight of inward anguish which no mortal could know. He was a man of sorrows and acquainted with grief. He looked forward to the accumulation of suffering which he knew would attend his last hours, with feelings on the rack of agony, with a heart exceedingly sorrowful even unto death, but with a meek and resigned resolution, a tender and trembling constancy, unspeakable superior in moral grandeur to the stern bravery of the proudest hero. In his last hours, with a bitterness of soul more excruciating than any bodily sufferings, he cried, "My God, my God, why hast thou forsaken me?" while yet, he promised heaven to a penitent fellow-sufferer, and died in an act of devotional confidence, triumphing that his work was finished. Thus he died, but rose again, that he might be the Lord of both the dead and the living; and he ascended to his Father and our Father, to his God and our God. This was the man Christ Jesus: a man demonstrated from God by miracles, and prodigies, and signs, which God did by him: a man ordained by God, to be the judge of the living and the dead.

Acts ii. 22.

Acts xvii. 31.

"It is delightful to dwell on the character of this unrivalled man: not only because in no other, since the foundation of the world, has the intellectual and moral perfection of our nature been exhibited, but because the contemplation of such excellence refreshes and elevates the mind, and encourages to the beneficial effort of imitation. He always did the things which pleased his heavenly Father. Love, zeal, purity, a perfect acquiescence in the Divine will on every occasion, and the most exalted habits of devotion, had their full place and exercise in his mind. The most refined generosity, but without affectation or display; mild-

ness, lowliness, tenderness, fidelity, candour, a delicate
respect for the feelings as well as the rights and interests of others, prudence, discriminating sagacity,
the soundest wisdom, and the noblest fortitude, shone
from this Son of righteousness with a lustre that never
was impaired."*

Believe me, we yield to none in the strength of conviction with which we hold to the humanity of Jesus
Christ. "The Word was made flesh, and dwelt among
us." We take our stand fearlessly on this. This un- John i. 14.
locks all those texts on which Unitarians are wont to
insist, asserting the inferiority and subordination of
the Son of man to the Father. We do not hide these
truths. We do not gloss them over. We do not ex-
plain them away. They are essential to our faith.
As combined with the revelations of his essential Godhead, they form that inimitable grace which is our
salvation. The foot of the ladder must rest on earth,
as the top of it reaches to heaven. Gen. xxviii. 12.
                                    John i. 51.

If our doctrine is the truth, that there subsist in the
essence of One Jehovah, three who are called the Father, the Son, and the Holy Spirit, coequal and co-
eternal; and that it is the design of the Father, and
the will of the Son, with the consenting pleasure of
the Holy Spirit, that the Son, for the recovery of
fallen man, should empty himself, not of his Deity,

---

* I make no apology for condensing and abstracting the two
preceding paragraphs from the profound treatise of Dr Pye
Smith, to which I have frequently referred, on "Scripture Testimony to the Messiah" (vol. ii. 334—337). Permit me to take
this opportunity of urging any who need a calm and candid investigation of this momentous subject, to study his noble apology
for our faith. Most thankful should I be, if my humble essay
formed the stepping-stone which should lead any to that truly
great work.

which were impossible, but of his glory, and take our human nature into mysterious union with his Divine nature, so that God and man make one Christ· if this is spoken of in Scripture as the extremity of Divine condescension, and humiliation, devised and accomplished, that hereby guilty men might have a medium of access to the Holy Deity,—or rather, foregoing abstract terms, that we might have a mediator betwixt us and God, one with God by reason of his eternal essence, one with us by reason of the humanity he deigned to assume; how otherwise could such a relationship have been expressed than in such or such like words—"There is one God and one mediator betwixt God and men, the man Christ Jesus; who gave himself a ransom for all?"—or such a salvation be described than, "This is life eternal, that they should know thee the only true God, and Jesus Christ whom thou hast sent?" Looking forward, as the man Christ Jesus, to his translation from this world of suffering to the glory of his Father's throne; (remember he had emptied himself, taken upon him the form of a servant, humbled himself—if these words mean anything, they imply a spontaneous descent from the higher to the lower;) how otherwise could he describe his return from that present estate of afflicted humanity, than in such or such like words—"If ye loved me, ye would rejoice, because I said, I go unto the Father; for my Father is greater than I?" Having descended with the express design of doing his Father's pleasure, of serving a perfect service, of rendering a spotless obedience to the law, of exhibiting a Divine model of self-denial; how otherwise could he declare his mission than in these or similar terms—"I came down from heaven, not to do mine own will, but the will of him that sent me?" Standing forth, the Author and

1 Tim. ii. 5, 6.

John xvii. 3.

John xiv. 28.

John vi. 38.

CHAP. V.

Finisher of the faith (τῆς πίστεως); the exemplar of that ^{Heb. xii. 2.} faith we are to copy; AS MAN, working his miracles not by virtue of his Divinity ever inherent in him, but by virtue of a perfect faith in the power of the Father; that faith which with us is intermittent and often overborne, being with him constant without defect, and victorious without defeat; how otherwise could he reveal the secret and entire dependence of his soul on God, than in language such as this,—"I can of mine own self do nothing.' "The Father that dwell- eth in me, he doeth the works?" ^{John v. 30; xiv. 10.}

(3) These passages affirm his proper humanity, and his humble mission as a servant. This humanity we assert as strongly, this mission we believe as verily as yourselves. All that faith requires is to act upon the great principle of comparing spiritual things with spiritual; and, wherever we find any assertion of his subordination as man, if we can place by its side a parallel assertion of his supremacy as God, faith de- mands nothing more. Often, the immediate context will supply the corrective, and adjust the balance. If not, we shall never consult in vain the whole counsel of the lively oracles of God.

Thus in the Old Testament, as man the seed of the woman is bruised in his heel: as God he achieves a victory surpassing human strength, he bruises the ^{Gen. iii. 15.} serpent's head. Against him as man, we read in the second Psalm, the kings of the earth set themselves: to him as the anointed Son of God, Divine royalty is ^{Ps. ii. 2, 7, 12.} ascribed and universal trust attracted. As man he appears at the close of the cxth Psalm, like a weary traveller, drinking of the wayside book and revived therewith; but the opening verses describe him as the victorious Lord of all on the throne with Jehovah. ^{Psa. cx. 1, 7.}

Isai. ix. 6.

If you regard his humanity, Unto us a child is born: if you regard his Deity, his name is the Mighty God. As David's son, he is the rod out of the stem of Jesse: as David's Lord, he shall smite the earth with the rod of his mouth, and with the breath of his lips shall he

Isai. xi. 1, 4.

slay the wicked. In respect of his manhood, he grows up as a tender plant, despised and rejected: in virtue of his Godhead, he bears the iniquity of us all, and

Isai. liii, 3, 6.

with his stripes we are healed. As man, he is the pierced, smitten shepherd: as God, he is Jehovah's

Zech. xii. 10; xiii. 7.

fellow.

And when we come to the New Testament, the evidence is yet more abundant. Space forbids to do more than place side by side, with a very few remarks, those Scriptures which reveal the characteristics of his manhood and his Godhead. Those on the left hand will record his functionary subordination as man; those on the right his essential supremacy as God:—

I came down from heaven not to do mine own will, but the will of him that sent me.—*John* vi. 38	Father, I will (θέλω)—*John* xvii. 24. The Son will (βούληται) to reveal him.—*Matt.* xi. 27.

His will, therefore, as man, was subjected to that of his Father: as God, was ever in perfect harmony with his Father's will, but was self-existent, free, efficacious.

Of that day and hour knoweth no man, no, not the angels which are in heaven, neither the Son, but the Father.—*Mark* xiii. 32.	The Father showeth the Son all things that himself doeth.—*John* v. 20. As the Father knoweth me, even so know I the Father.—*John* x. 15. Lord, thou knowest all things. —*John* xxi. 17.

Luke ii. 52

Just as we read, Jesus increased in wisdom, and therefore there were subjects unknown to him at twelve years of age, which were acquired by him or revealed to him afterwards: so in Mark xiii. 32, Jesus is speaking in his human nature. This point was not made known to him as man, by the Spirit. And since his manhood is spoken of as a condition of his prophetical office (Deut. xviii. 15, *of thy brethren*) he is declaring as an ambassador, what lay within his commission, and this day and hour he was not empowered, as Prophet, to reveal.* The contrast verses sufficiently prove he

---

* I think we may safely draw here a parallel betwixt the omnipotence and omniscience of Christ. We have seen (p. 96, 97) that no exception can be taken against his Almighty power as God from the words, "I can of mine own self do nothing;" because, *as man*, he wrought his miracles, not by virtue of his Deity, which was ever inherent in him, but by virtue of a perfect faith in the power of the Father, through the plenitude of the Holy Ghost. Though as God ever and always able to do all things, he, of his own Divine will, resolved not to exert this personal omnipotence betwixt his incarnation and his crucifixion. This resolution was part of the κένωσις spoken of, Phil. ii. 7. Therefore, with respect to the exertion of power, by his spontaneous act of self-emptying, "the Son was able to do nothing of himself." His might was his Father's might. And the mean of its exertion was his own unfaltering faith. We have an illustrious example of this in his thanksgiving prayer, when raising Lazarus from the dead:—"Father, I thank thee that thou hast heard me. And I knew that thou hearest me always." John xi. 41, 42. So with regard to this other attribute of Deity, omniscience. No exception against his infinite wisdom, as God, can justly be taken from the words, "The Son knoweth not that day or hour." At his incarnation, he of his own accord resolved not to use, *as man*, during the days of his humiliation, the knowledge which his omniscience as God would afford. That resolution again was part of the κένωσις. The wisdom he used was the illumination of the Spirit given to him without measure. The means of its acquirement were diligence and prayer.

All human illustrations of this great mystery must fail. But have we not heard in chivalry of a warrior, in order to meet a partially disabled adversary on equal terms, allowing his own right arm to hang unemployed by his side? Have we not heard in

shared the infinite counsels of his Father, comprehended the Incomprehensible, and is himself Omniscient.

---

diplomacy of an ambassador, with sealed instructions which he is
only to open at his discretion, conducting a negotiation without
knowing the mind of the senate he represents, though the means
of knowing it were ready to his hand in his portfolio? That warrior could use his arm, and yet by his own resolution he could not
use it. That ambassador could break the seals, and yet in the
best exercise of his judgment he could not do so. The one would
truthfully declare, "I cannot stretch forth the right hand of my
power;" and the other, "I do not know the counsels of my state."
The one fights as if he had no right arm; and the other negotiates
as if the will of his country had not been confided to his keeping.
I offer these illustrations with much diffidence, knowing how far
short every earthly, figure of these heavenly mysteries must fall.
But if it be possible for finite man in all sincerity to declare, when
physically able, "I cannot act," and when the means of knowledge
are his, "I do not know;" how much rather may these things be
in the mission of the Infinite Son of God!'

There are precipices on the right hand and on the left. Let us
not go a hair's breadth beyond the declarations of Scripture: but
at the same time let us accept, with confidence and candour, all
those declarations. From everlasting to everlasting, before, during, and after his humiliation, Jesus Christ was, and is, and is to
come, the Lord God Omnipotent and Omniscient. "Power belongeth unto God," Psa. lxii. 11. "Wisdom and might are his," Dan,
ii. 20. They are the inalienable attributes of Deity. They could
never be laid aside. They could never cease to exist in God.
But we must not confound *non-existence* and *non-exertion*. Thus
the patriarch argues, "Will he plead against me with his great
power? No," Job xxiii. 6. Thus the Psalmist records, "He did
not stir up all his wrath," Psa. lxxviii. 38. And thus the prophet
solaces us, "He stayeth his rough wind in the day of the east
wind," Isai. xxvii. 8. These words indicate that Jehovah did not
put forth all his almightiness and all his holy indignation. That
is to say, to use the language of men, that these attributes were
in part unexcited or unexerted. Omnipotence restraining itself
is not therefore a view of the actings of Deity unwarranted by

I go unto the Father; for my Father is greater than I.—*John* xiv. 28.

Making himself equal with God.—*John* v. 18. With our Lord's consequent discourse, ver. 19—29. (See pp. 81, 82.)

Inferiority of rank as man, as mediator, as the apostle and servant of his Father—having for us spontaneously stooped from the throne of his glory—is asserted in the first quotation: equality of nature as to co-operation, self-existence, infinite knowledge, universal trust, is proved in the second.

The very texts which most strongly declare the humanity of Jesus, are sufficient, as Coleridge somewhere observes, to refute those who from them would deny

---

Scripture. Why then should we be stumbled at these expressions of the God-man regarding himself?

Nay, so far from being staggered at these things, the considerations, which they suggest, are of the utmost value when we contemplate Jesus, as our example: "Who in the days of his flesh offered up prayers and supplications with strong crying and tears to him that' was able to save him from death; who was in all points tempted like as we are; and who in that he has suffered being tempted is able to succour them that are tempted," Heb. ii. 18; iv. 15; v. 7. He put himself as far as possible on a level with us for "in all things it behoved him to be made like unto his brethren," Heb. ii. 17. We feel all the suasive attraction of sympathy. We acknowledge all the power of the example of our elder Brother. We may draw from the same Fountain from whence the man Christ Jesus drew. The way of access through his blood is open to us. The Spirit is willing to strengthen us with might in the inner man. Yea, God in Christ is himself our wisdom and our strength. We have all the consolations of his perfect humanity; but these truths do not minish aught from his perfect Divinity. Nay, they glorify it with new beauties, where we see how, in the weakness of human flesh but in the might of Divine faith, how, in the gradual development of human powers but in the full enlightment of the Divine Spirit, his absolute indefectible goodness, the goodness of infinite love, proved him to be the only-begotten of the Father, God of God, Light of light, very God of very God.

his Deity. How could a mere man, without absurd presumption, solemnly announce that God the Father was greater than he? How could he be made flesh? How could it be a proof of his humility that he was made in the likeness of man?

This may be the fittest opportunity to say a few words on the answer of Christ to the ruler, "Why callest thou me good? There is none good but one, that is, God; but if thou wilt enter into life, keep the commandments." This young man, coming to Christ and exclaiming, "Good teacher, what good thing (διδάσκαλε ἀγαθέ, τί ἀγαθόν) shall I do that I may have eternal life?" manifestly only recognized him as a human teacher; as such, called him good; nay, put his own good works on the same level of merit. The Lord refused such homage. It was founded on false assumptions. Its acceptance would have strengthened a yet unhumbled self-righteousness. "Why," he asked, "why callest thou me good?" The stress is on the "why." The answer to that "why," would discover an unsuspected depth of self-ignorance. But the Lord proceeded to probe the young man's heart, and tried him by the second table of the law wherein he rested. The ruler was found wanting. We know not his after history; but thus, at least, one barrier was broken down which, unremoved, must have ever kept him from confessing his need of an atonement for sin, from imploring the advocacy of Jesus Christ the righteous, and from trusting in the perfect goodness of him, before whom unconsciously then he knelt, Jehovah our righteousness. But to resume.

Matt. xix. 16, 17.

To sit on my right hand, and on my left, is not mine to give, except to those for whom it is prepared of my Father.—*Matt.* xx. 23.

To him that overcometh will I grant to sit with me in my throne.—*Rev.* iii. 21.

The translation given above of our Lord's reply to Salome simply omits the words which are not in the original.* The promise to the church of Laodicea sufficiently proves that, in respect of heavenly dignities, Jesus Christ does as he wills with his own.

God so loved the world, that he gave his only-begotten Son. —*John* iii. 16.

Christ also loved the church, and gave himself for her.—*Eph.* v. 25.

It pleased the Lord to bruise him; he hath put him to grief: when thou shalt make his soul an offering for sin.—*Isai.* liii. 10.

I lay down my life that I might take it again. No one οὐδείς taketh it from me. I have power † to lay it down, and I have power to take it again.— *John* x. 17, 18.

Whom God hath raised up, having loosed the pains of death. —*Acts* ii. 24.

Destroy this temple (his body), and in three days I will raise it up.—*John* ii. 19.

He (the Father of glory) set him at his own right hand in the heavenly places, far above all principality and power.— *Eph.* i. 20, 21.

He ascended up on high, he led captivity captive.—*Eph.* iv. 8. Having spoiled principalities and powers, he made a show of them openly.—*Col.* ii. 15.

In these passages you will observe that, on the one hand, the death, resurrection, and ascension of Jesus as man, being subordinate to the Father and at his disposal, are said to have taken place at his Father's ordination: while on the other hand, as God, Christ gives himself, raises himself, ascends in his own might, and as the King of glory, the Lord of hosts mighty in battle, enters the everlasting doors.

---

* Cf. Scholefield's "Hints," and Alford; and for construction ἀλλ' οἷς ἡτοίμασται compare precisely similar idiom in the previous chapter, ver. 11, ἀλλ' οἷς δέδοται, where it is properly translated "save."

† Unitarians object to ἐξουσία being here translated "power," (they would prefer "authority,") but it is so rendered of the Father's power, Luke xii. 5; Acts i. 7, and (as they would add) Jude 25. The previous clause declares the spontaneity of the gift.

And now, Lord.....grant.... | Aeneas, Jesus Christ maketh
that signs and wonders may be | thee whole.—*Acts* ix. 34.
done by the name of thy holy
child Jesus.—*Acts* iv. 29, 30.

If the first exalts the Father, the second, as distinctly, exalts the Son as the immediate Author of miraculous healing.

Forgiving one another, even | Forgiving one another, even
as God for Christ's sake hath for- | as Christ forgave you.—*Col.* iii.
given you.—*Eph.* iv. 32. | 13.

Now the Father, now the Son, is referred to as the first cause of forgiveness.

To us (there is but) one God | And one Lord Jesus Christ,
the Father, of whoim (ἐξ οὖ) are | by whom (δι' οὖ) are all things,
all things, and we unto (εἰς) him. | and we by him.—1 *Cor.* viii. 6.
1 *Cor.* viii. 6. |

On this, Dr. P. Smith says, "Lord is not put as a designation secondary and inferior to God. It attributes dominion; and the extent of the domin oni must be according to the nature of the case in any given instance. Is there anything, then, in this case to direct our conception? Yes: all things are 'by him,' or 'through him,' as their immediate and efficient Cause. The identical phrase is used, which is twice by the same writer employed with regard to the Eternal Father (Rom. xi. 36; Heb. ii. 10): by whom (δι' οὖιτὰ πάντα) are all things." To me who believe the reference to be to Deut. vi. 4, as stated p. 76, no proof could be stronger than this of the Divine Supremacy of the Messiah. But at all events, "the *Deity* of Christ can no more be denied, because the Father is here called the 'One God,' than the *dominion* of the Father can be denied, because the Son is called the 'One Lord.' "*

---

*There are two other passages to which Unitarians sometimes refer, but the deduction they draw from them is, in each case, refuted by the context.

Ye are Christ's; and Christ is God's.—1 *Cor.* iii. 23.

The head of Christ is God.—1 *Cor.* xi. 3.

Then cometh the end, when he shall have delivered up the kingdom to God, even the Father; . . . .

Then shall the Son also himself be subject unto him that

I am in the Father, and the Father in me.—*John* xiv. 10.

He the (Son) is the head of the body, the church.—*Col.* i. 18.

Of his (Christ's) kingdom there shall be no end.—*Luke* i. 33.

The everlasting kingdom of our Lord and Saviour Jesus Christ.—2 *Peter* i. 11.

Thy throne, O God, is for ever and ever. . . . . Thou art the

(1) "The first-born of all creation" πρωτότοχος πάσης κτίσεως, or "of the whole creation."—*Col.* i. 15.

But the apostle continues—

"For by him were all things created." ver. 16.

If you regard the word *first-born* in its general acceptation among Eastern nations, it imports lordship, excellence, dignity; and as such the clause might well have been translated here, "The chief of all creation." But if you press for a more exact significance, it absolutely resists the interpretation that Christ is himself a creation of God, for then it would have been πρωτόχτιστος first created, as Chrysostom observes (see Scott), not πρωτότοχος first-born. The (-τοχος) guards this, and the πρωτο- so far from assuming him to be the *first* creature, declares his pre-existent priority to all creation, according to the well-known Greek usage of the superlative for the comparative, (see John i. 15, ὅτι πρῶτός μου ἦν, for he was before me)ι and the clause might have been rendered by that in our version of the Athanasian creed: "Begotten before the worlds." Thus the phrase by itself is an unambiguous testimony to his Deity; and the succeeding clauses, ascribing to him the creation of all, prove him increate; for, if a creature, he made himself, which is absurd.

(2) The beginning of the creation of God, ἡ ἀρχὴ—*Rev.* iii. 14.

Compare with this, "I am, saith the Lord, the beginning and the end" ἡ ἀρχή χαὶ τὸ τέλος)—*Rev.* i. 8; xxi. 6; xxii. 13.

The above comprise all the instances of the use of ἀρχὴ in the Apocalypse, and sufficiently prove that, as used in chap. iii. 14, it regards the pre-existent eternity, the "from everlasting" of the Lord, and as such declares him to be the beginning or origin, or originator, or precisely as we say, *the First Cause* of the creation of God.

put all things under him, that God may be all in all.—1 *Cor.* xv. 24, 28.	same. . . . Sit on my right hand.—*Heb.* i. 8, 12, 13. Christ is all and in all.—*Col.* iii. 11.

From these passages, on the one side, we learn that Jesus Christ as the last Adam, the federal Head of his church, in ascending to our God and Father has ascended to his God and Father; and that as our surety he does his Father's will; and that a time will come when he will no longer exercise his mediatorial office, by pleading the virtue of his blood for penitent sinners (seeing that sin and death are for ever abolished); but as the representative of us, his blood-bought children, (for the memory of his dying love shall never fade throughout eternity,) will keep his Father's commandments and abide in his love; and that thus for ever and for ever Jehovah shall fill the universe with the unclouded effulgence of his everlasting name and essence, LOVE. On the other hand, we learn that Christ and his Father are one; that he has a real and undivided supremacy; that his kingdom shall never wax old, his glory never pale, his royalty never pass away; and that for the endless ages of immortality in heaven and earth, the manifestation of the love of God shall be through him, who is the brightness of his Father's glory, and is seated on the right hand of the Majesty on high.

I append only one couplet more; for the same principle applies to all the passages which have been, or can be, brought forward to prove the subordination of the Son.

In the midst of the throne and of the four living creatures, and in the midst of the elders, stood a Lamb as it had been slain.—*Rev.* v. 6.	A pure river of water of life, clear as crystal, proceeding out of the throne of God and of the Lamb.—*Rev.* xxii. 1.

Do you gather from the first passage that in Christ glorified there are ineffaceable traces of Jesus and him crucified?—from the last you learn that the perennial and transparent stream of felicity—the joy of the Holy Ghost—flows equally and co-ordinately from the eternal Father and the eternal Son.

I have now, I believe, brought forward the principal of those passages on which Unitarians rely. Is there any thing in any one of them, or in all collectively, to prevent our reposing supreme confidence in Jesus Christ?—do they rebuke our absolute dependence upon him?—do they warn us against loving him with every affection of our soul?

The Scriptures, adduced in the last two chapters, brought before us one of such Divine perfections, that, if he were not God, not the object of supreme reliance, we should at least have needed a caveat every few lines—"Art thou tempted to worship him? See thou do it not. Though the instrument, he is not the author of eternal salvation. Though Godlike, he is not God. Though wearing vice-regal honours, he is not king. Be on your guard. Control your feelings. Curb your affections. Moderate your admiration. Keep your trust in check. He is only a creature after all. Beware of idolatry; and again I say, beware." Now I ask, do the passages, affirming his subordination as man, contain that caveat—or anything like such a warning?—or any, even the faintest, intimation, of the possibility of loving him too much, or trusting in him too entirely? You must confess they do not. Yea more, as you stoop down and look into these mysteries of his humiliation, they touch deeper and deeper springs within you, they awaken the finer sensibilities of your nature; and when you believe that he, who was in the form of God, emptied himself for you, and took upon him the form of a servant, confidence and affection alike reach a standard that nothing can transcend. You trust him, you love him, you adore him supremely, for that exceeding great and costly love wherewith he loved you, and gave himself for you.

And now every generous feeling within you brands it as the basest ingratitude to allege these proofs of his humanity in disproof of his Deity, to trample on his lowliness that you may pluck the diadem from his brow, and to find cause in the true sympathy of him who was in all points tempted like as we are, and touched with the feeling of our infirmities, for denying the excellence of that glory which he had with the Father before the world was. If a sick and suffering prisoner in Newgate, nursed, and tended, and taught, by the philanthropic Howard, had argued, from the self-devotion of that noble man spending long hours in the loathsome cell, that he could not possess a princely mansion, and fortune of his own; and even if he had reproached that ministering angel, saying, "You must surely be a wretched convict like myself," we might pity his infatuation and pardon his ingratitude:—but can we forgive ourselves, if we deliberately select the instances of our Lord's lowest humiliation and cast them in his teeth, as proving that he never dwelt from eternity in the light that no man can approach unto, nor inhabited from everlasting that shrine of unfathomable delights, the bosom of his Father? Let us beware, my friends, and remember the solemn warning of Jesus, "Whosoever shall fall on this stone (himself in prostrate humility) shall be broken; but on whomsoever it shall fall, (himself returning in glory,) it will grind him to powder."

(4) The Word was made flesh. Oh, wondrous humiliation of the Creator! But this is not all. "He came," and "as many as received him, to them gave he power to become the sons of God." Oh wondrous exaltation of us his creatures! They are two mysteries, of which the second is only less marvellous than the first. He, the Infinite One, stooped to the extremity of woe that he might elevate us to the highest life which a created being can enjoy—the life of God. And this explains another series of truths, which I blush for myself and for human nature to confess once troubled my peace, and is I know at the present moment darkening the faith of many: I mean the exalted expressions which Scripture contains of our privileges in Christ. *John i. 11, 12.*

What argument, UNBELIEF SUGGESTS, can you draw from the infinite mutual love of the Father and the Son, when Jesus says, "As the Father loved me, *so have I loved you*"?— *John xv. 9.*

Or from the infinite knowledge possessed by the Son of the Father, when he says, "No one knoweth the Father, save the Son, *and he to whomsoever the Son will reveal him*"?— *Matt. xi. 27.*

Or from the Son being the express image of his person, when it is said, *"we are changed into the same image from glory to glory"*?— *2 Cor. iii. 18.*

Or from his Divine nature as the Son of God, when *"we are joint heirs with him who is the first-born among many brethren, and are ourselves partakers of a Divine nature"*?— *Rom. viii. 17, 29. 2 Pet. i. 4.*

Or from his words, "I and my Father are one," when he prays for his people *"that they may be one even as we are one"*?— *John xvii. 22.*

Or from his own mighty miracles, when he promises

CHAP. V.

his faithful disciple, *"Greater works than these* (of mine) *shall he do"?*—

John xiv. 12.

Or from his session on the eternal throne, when he says, *we shall share his throne?*—

Rev. iii. 21.

Or from his saying, "He that hath seen me hath seen the Father," when he also says, *He that heareth you heareth me?*—

Luke x. 16.

Or from his assurance, "As the Father knoweth me even so know I the Father," when Paul says in the confidence of faith, *"Then shall I know even as also I am known"?*

1 Cor. xiii. 12.

Or from the infinite comprehension implied in the words, "The Father showeth the Son all things that himself doeth," when Jesus says, *"All things that I have heard of my Father I have made known unto you"?*—

John xv. 15.

Or from the name of Jesus, "The Saviour of the world, who shall save his people from their sins," when among the Old Testament saints we find there were *"saviours, who saved them;"* when Paul says, *"I became all things to all men, that I might by all means save some;"* and when James avers, *"He that converteth a sinner from the error of his way shall save a soul from death"?*—

Neh. ix. 27.

1 Co. ix. 22.

James v. 20.

Or from the express definition, "The Word was God," when Christ declares, *"He called them gods, unto whom the word of God came"?*—

John x. 35.

Or from the solemn affirmation, "In him dwelleth all the fulness of the Godhead bodily," when Scripture records the prayer, *"that ye might be filled even to all the fulness of God"?*

Eph. iii. 19.

Oh base unbelief! Oh hateful suspicion! If I have done wrong in giving consistent expression to thoughts, which have been flung as fiery darts against the shield of faith, the Lord pardon his servant in this thing.

But the answer is conclusive, and the suggestion un-
answered may rankle in many breasts. I do not now
insist on the exceeding ingratitude of the return—to
take advantage of the infinite love of Christ and say,
the believer is advanced to so high a dignity, and is
admitted to such Divine delights, there can surely be
no difference betwixt him and the eternal Son of God;
but, I ask, what saith the Scripture to this objection
of the glories of Christ, and of his redeemed, being
from time to time described in apparently similar
terms?

In the first place, most of the attributes and names
of Christ are never predicated of his people: they are
his own essential prerogatives: they are incommunicable. Then if we take up one by one those passages
whose force is thought to be neutralized by the corresponding privileges of saints, we shall see how, in
each case, the privilege of the believer is derived from
Christ, or from the Father through Christ, (the context
compelling this,) and is limited by the finite capacity
of the creature; while the supereminent glory of Christ
is either underived, eternal, increate,—or, if given, is
expressly given to him in his subordinate character as
Mediator. And, lastly, no pretension of trust in any
saint or saints is founded on the privileges conferred
on him or them in the gospel.

As to the first point, you may easily verify it for
yourself, by referring to chapters iii. and iv. Where
is any saint said to be the only-begotten Son of God,
the First and the Last, from everlasting, the same yesterday, to-day, and for ever, omnipresent, omniscient,
infinitely good, the Creator and Preserver of all things,
the chief Shepherd of the flock, the one Master and
Lord, the Bridegroom of the bride, Jehovah? Nowhere.
Therefore setting these disputed passages aside for a

while, even without them the proof remains incontrovertible.

Secondly, let us examine this alleged similarity
more closely. But to deprecate a hasty conclusion from
a bare resemblance of words, I would remind you,
there are a few instances in Scripture in which the
same phrase denotes a prerogative of the Supreme
Father, and a privilege of his believing child. Thus
Matt. xix. 26. we find, "With God all things are possible." And
Mark ix. 23. again, "All things are possible to him that believeth."
Would you, because of the sameness of the terms employed, deny the omnipotence of God, or ascribe omnipotence to the believer? Again, "Be ye therefore
Matt. v. 48. perfect, even as your Father which is in heaven is perfect." Would you, because of the prefection of the
saint, deny the infinite goodness of the Father; or
because of the absolute perfection of the Father, ascribe
illimitable goodness to the saint? Here, indeed,
Prov. xiv. 6. "Knowledge is easy unto him that understandeth."
Let us, however, proceed to examine them:—

The Father loveth the Son, and hath given all things unto his hands. He that believeth on the Son hath everlasting life. —*John* iii. 35, 36.

As the Father hath loved me, so have I loved you: continue ye in my love. If ye keep my commandments, ye shall abide in my love.—*John* xv. 9, 10.

In the first quotation, supreme authority is assigned
to Christ, as the heir of all things for his church;
and the trust of mankind centres on him. In the
second, he is urging his disciples as defectible beings,
by the plea of the infinite fulness of his love towards
them, infinite so far as regarded himself, to abide in
that love, from which without him they would assuredly fall, "for without me," as he had just said,
John xv. 5. "ye can do nothing."

All things are delivered unto me of my Father: and no one knoweth the Son, but the Father; neither knoweth any one the Father, save the Son.—*Matt.* xi. 27.

And he to whomsoever the Son will reveal him.—*Matt.* xi. 27.

The first part is again accompanied by the declaration of the Son's unlimited inheritance of all things. The second is qualified by the previous assertion that these things were revealed to babes, and their finite knowledge of the Father is granted through the Son, as the efficient cause.

The express image of his person.—*Heb.* i. 3.

Changed into the same image, —*2 Cor.* iii. 18.

The first clause is extracted from that chapter which so illustriously proves the Deity of Christ. The second refers all the transformation to the view "of the glory of God in the face of Jesus Christ," revealed ² Cor. iv. 6. progressively by the Lord, the Spirit.

Unto which of the angels said he at any time, Thou art my Son, this day have I begotten thee?—*Heb.* i. 5.

Sons of God.
Joint heirs with Christ.

[The first-born,] among many brethren.—*Rom.* viii. 14, 17, 29.

We have here another testimony to Christ, which connects itself with all those passages affirming that in a sense peculiar to himself he is the Son of God; standing forth as the Son, the only-begotten of the Father, the Son of his love, his own Son, the Son of the living God, the Son of the Blessed, the Son of the Highest. From a cursory glance into the eighth of Romans, we see how infinite the difference betwixt that essential Sonship, and our privileges, as adopted sons, which are only ours in Christ; and thus it is, as Peter writes, through the righteousness of our God and Saviour, Jesus Christ, through the knowledge of God and

John i. 14
Col. i. 13
Rom. viii. 32
Matt. xvi. 16
Mark xiv. 61
Luke i. 32

of Jesus our Lord, that we become partakers of a (not *the*) Divine nature.

I and my Father are one.— *John* x. 30.	That they may be one, even as we are one.—*John* xvii. 22.

On the first hangs the security of the church universal, which is safe, whether held in his hand, or, to vary the aspect of truth, held in his Father's hand; equally safe, for he and his Father are one in essence, power, operation, and will. From the second, we learn how intimate is the union of the saints with each other, and the Lord; but, unutterably glorious as are the privileges besought by Christ for his people in that sublime prayer, they all flow equally from the Father, and from himself, (v. 3) as the one fountain of eternal life.

The works that I do in my Father's name bear witness of me.—*John* x. 25.	Greater works than these shall he do.—*John* xiv. 12.

In the former, the works are appealed to as proof of his right to be the Shepherd of his flock, and the Messiah of Israel. In the latter, all the miracles, as he had just stated, are wrought by faith in him: "he that believeth on me, the works that I do shall he do also."

To the Son he saith, Thy throne, O God, is for ever and ever.—*Heb.* i. 8.	To him that overcometh will I grant to sit with me in my throne.—*Rev.* iii. 21.

It only needs the collation of the verses, to see the immeasurable difference betwixt the universal supremacy belonging of right to Christ for ever, and the favour granted by him to his people of reigning with him.

He that hath seen me hath seen the Father.—*John* xiv. 9.	He that heareth you heareth me.—*Luke* x. 16.

The first explains how knowledge of himself embraces knowledge of the Father, and vindicates his claim to be "the way, and the truth, and the life." The second clothes his messengers with an ambassador's official authority, as speaking *in loco regis.*

As the Father knoweth me, even so know I the Father.— *John* x. 15.	Then shall I know even as also I am known.—1 *Cor.* xiii. 12.

The good Shepherd, who is to know thoroughly all his sheep, needs omniscience; this, the first proves. *John x. 14.* From the second, we are assured that in heaven our knowledge will be not fragmentary as here, but *so far as it extends,* will resemble Christ's knowledge of us, being perfect, symmetrical, unperplexed.

The Father showeth the Son all things that himself doeth.— *John* v. 20.	All things that I have heard of my Father, I have made known unto you.—*John* xv. 15.

The first is accompanied (see p. 82) with every Divine claim. The second is qualified by the quickly succeeding assurance, "I have yet many things to say unto you, but ye cannot bear them now." *John xvi. 12.*

Christ, the Saviour of the world. *John* iv. 42.	Thou gavest them saviours, who saved them.— *Neh.* ix. 27.
Jesus, who delivered us from the wrath to come.—1 *Thess.* i. 10.	He that converteth a sinner .... shall save a soul from death.—*James* v. 20.

It needs only a glance at the parallel passages, (pages 43, 44,) to see how infinite is the difference betwixt him who stands forth emphatically the Author of eternal salvation, and those who were deliverers of their country from oppression, or were instruments as the ministers of Jesus Christ in the salvation of souls.

The Word was God.—*John* i. 1.	He called them gods, to whom the word of God came.—*John* x. 35.

In the first, the context compels us to understand (Θεός) God, when applied to the Word, in the same sense as when immediately before and after applied to the Father: the Word is essentially God, the Creator of all. The second, conceding indeed that there is a

Ps. lxxxii. 6, 7.

lower sense in which men were sometimes officially *called* gods, (though the passage adduced marks their mortality—they shortly die like other men,) contrasts with this the Divine Sonship of the Messiah.

| In him dwelleth all the fulness of the Godhead bodily.— *Col.* ii. 9. | That ye might be filled even to all (εἰς πᾶν) the fulness of God. —*Eph.* iii. 19. |

The first affirms the incarnate Deity of Christ as the One in whom (see next clause, v. 10) we are complete, for he is the head of all principality and power. The second (somewhat obscured by the received translation) imports that we may be filled "each in our degree and to the utmost bound of our finite capacity, even as God is full, with Divine goodness:" and this again flows from our knowledge of the illimitable love of Christ.

The difficulties, when fairly tried by the context in each case, crumble into dust; and the formidable line of objections founded on them melt, like embankments of snow, when exposed to the full light of other Scriptures which assert the true Deity of the Son.

But now, I ask, do these contrasted truths divert us from reposing supreme trust in Jesus Christ? Do they, even so far as this, confuse our confidence, by setting up any other as the recipient of equal honour? Because the saints are loved with Divine love, know God, are changed into his image, are called his sons, are made one with the Father and with Christ, work mighty works by his power, are raised to Christ's throne, shall hereafter possess a perfect knowledge, are made acquainted with the mysteries of gospel grace, may even officially be called gods, and, what is a far higher privilege, be filled with all Divine goodness,— is any claim set up on their behalf for trust or worship? Gather together all the privileges of Christians here set forth; entwine them into one radiant crown; place that crown, as you are prefectly warranted in doing, upon the head of some eminent saipt, Peter, or Paul, or John, or even of the church catholic, the Bride, is there in all these lustrous glories any temptation held out to confide in absolutely, or supremely to love, that saint, or that church?

We acknowledge the extremity of abasement to which Jesus descended. We believe the summit of glory to which he will raise his people. We accept the simple declarations of Scripture with regard to both these facts. But for a man to take his stand alternately on the lowest step of Christ's humiliation, and on the highest step of his children's exaltation, and thence to deny the Supreme Deity of him who stooped so low that he might draw us up so high, seems an ingratitude of which our dealings with our fellow-men afford no parallel.

We referred before to the opening of the Epistle to the Ephesians—Scripture does not contain a more rich See p. 36. exhibition of those things which are ours in Christ. Now if Paul had closed that chapter by arrogating Christ-like honours or Christ-like homage to himself and his brethren, there would have been some ground for alarm that the dignities of his people were eclipsing the supremacy of their Lord. How different is the spirit breathed through his glowing prayer!—

"That the God of our Lord Jesus Christ, the Father of glory, may give unto you the spirit of wisdom and revelation in the knowledge of him; the eyes of your understanding being enlightened; that ye may know what is the hope of his calling, and what the riches of the glory of his inheritance in the saints, and what is the exceeding greatness of his power to us-ward who believe, according to the working of his mighty power, which he wrought in Christ, when he raised him from the dead, and set him at his own right hand in the heavenly places, far above all principality, and power, and might, and dominion, and every name that is named, not only in this world, but also in that which is to come; and hath put all things under his feet, and gave him to be the head over all things to the church, which is his body, the fulness of him that Eph. i. 17–23. filleth all in all."

Behold, the Son is on the everlasting throne: and we are under his feet. Moved indeed by Divine compassion, he once forsook that throne, and came forth from the bosom of his Father, that he might gather together the children of God which are scattered abroad, and present them as one family before the presence of his glory with exceeding joy. Is your trust weakened in him because of his exceeding humiliation? or do you think the less of him for the glory to which he elevates his people? Nay, verily: gratitude can find no words to express itself when we believe on him who, being "over all, God blessed for ever," partook of our flesh and blood, and now seated far above all principality and power, is not ashamed to Heb. ii. 11.   call us brethren.

CHAPTER VI

AND now I would state my next proposition, and briefly sketch the testimony on which it rests:

That Scripture, in the Old and the New Testament alike, proves the coequal Godhood of the Holy Spirit with that of the Father and of the Son.

May the same Spirit grant us reverence, and humility, and godly fear in this solemn inquiry.

The reader will not fail to observe what strong collateral evidence of the possible plurality in unity, and therefore of the possible coequal Deity of the Father and of the Son, we shall obtain, if another be revealed in Scripture;

> as one who is to be distinguished from the Father and the Son;
>
> as one to whom such personal properties and actions are assigned as prove independent and intelligent personality;
>
> as one to whom Divine attributes are ascribed, and by whom Divine offices are exercised;
>
> as one worshipped in parity with the Father and the Son;
>
> as one declared to be Jehovah and God.

Here indeed we might expect the evidence to be more subjective; for the peculiar office of the Holy Ghost in the economy of redemption, is ever represented as the quickening and fostering of the hidden life within. It is, however, none the less conclusive. If, as we gaze on the sun shining in the firmament, we see any faint adumbration of the doctrine of the Trinity in the fontal orb, the light ever generated, the heat proceeding from the sun and its beams—three-fold and yet one, the sun, its light, and its heat—that luminous globe, and the radiance ever flowing from it, are both evident to the eye; but the vital warmth is felt, not seen, and is only manifested in the life it transfuses through creation. The proof of its real existence is self-demonstrating.

(1) That the Divine Spirit is to be distinguished from the Father and the Son, appears from all those passages in Holy Scripture, which reveal to us the simultaneous co-operation of three infinite agents.

Thus when we read, at our Lord's baptism, of the voice of the Father, of the human presence of Jesus, of the visible descent of the Spirit, for "the heaven was opened, and the Holy Ghost descended in a bodily shape like a dove upon him, and a voice came from heaven, which said, Thou art my beloved Son: in thee I am well pleased:"—we are compelled to say, that the descending Spirit is distinct from the baptized Saviour, and from the approving Father.

Luke iii. 21, 22.

And when Jesus says, "I wiil pray the Father, and he shall give you another Comforter, that he may abide with you for ever;" and when, this promise being fulfilled on the day of Pentecost, we find that the Holy Ghost appeared seated on the disciples as cloven tongues of fire; we are constrained to acknowledge that the apparent Spirit is distinct from the mediating Saviour, and the Father who decreed the gift.

John xiv. 16.

Acts ii. 3.

And when we read of "the name of the Father, and of the Son, and of the Holy Ghost," and again of "the grace of the Lord Jesus Christ, and the love of God, and the fellowship of the Holy Spirit," it is impossible to deny the necessary distinction here affirmed.

Matt. xxviii. 19.

2 Cor. xiii. 14.

And when the saints are described as "elect according to the fore-knowledge of God the Father, through sanctification of the Spirit, unto obedience and sprinkling of the blood of Jesus Christ," Scripture leads us to conclude that as the bleeding Saviour is distinct from the predestinating Father, so the sanctifying Spirit is himself distinct.

1 Pet. i. 2.

And when the benediction of grace and peace is implored from (ἀπὸ) him which is, and which was, and which is to come; and from (καὶ ἀπὸ) "the seven spirits which are before the throne;* and from (καὶ ἀπὸ)

Rev. i. 4, 5.

---

* The phrase is emblematical, but not the less definitive and precise when compared with other Scriptures. Indeed, emblems

Jesus Christ, the faithful witness," we are assured that
as there is a distinction intended between the eternal

---

are a kind of universal language for every age and country. After
all that has been written on this subject, I feel persuaded that
the word is here its own interpreter. The principal passages
bearing on this are—

(1) "The Spirit of Jehovah shall rest upon him; the spirit of
wisdom and understanding, the spirit of counsel and might, the
spirit of knowledge and of the fear of Jehovah, and shall make him
of quick understanding in the fear of Jehovah." I do not think ^{Isai. xi. 2, 3.}
any stress can be laid on the *number* here, as the Hebrew only
enumerates six, repeating the last with a preposition—(Though
the Septuagint distinguishes seven, πνεῦμα σοφίας—συνέσεως,—βου-
λῆς, —ἰσχύος,—γνώσεως,—εὐσεβείας,—adding as the seventh, πνεῦμα φόβου Θεοῦ)—but on the *multiplicity* of perfections designated
by various names and compromised in one, the Spirit of Jehovah.

(2) "Upon one stone shall be seven eyes." ^{Zech. iii. 9.}

"Those seven; they are the eyes of Jehovah, which run to and
fro through the whole earth. The Septuagint translates the ^{Zech. iv. 10.}
seven in the same clause with the eyes, ἑπτὰ οὗτοι ὀφθαλμοί εἰσιν
οἱ ἐπιβλέποντες ἐπὶ πᾶσαν τὴν γῆν.

(3) "And from the seven Spirits which are before his throne." ^{Rev. i. 4.}

(4) "These things saith he that hath the seven Spirits of God." ^{Rev. iii. 1.}

(5) "And seven lamps of fire, burning before the throne, which
are the seven spirits of God." ^{Rev. iv. 5.}

(6) "In the midst of the throne and of the four living creatures,
and in the midst of the elders, stood a Lamb as it had been slain,
having seven horns and seven eyes, which are the seven Spirits
of God sent forth into all the earth" (ὀφθαλμούς, ἑπτὰ οἵ εἰσι τὰ ἑπτὰ ^{Rev. v. 6.}
τοῦ Θεοῦ πνεύματα τὰ ἀπεσταλμένα εἰς πᾶσαν τὴν γῆν). No one can fail
remarking the designed coincidence betwixt this and the Septuagint version, given above, of Zech. iv. 10.

Here we learn,

from (3) and (5) *the distinction* to be observed between God
and the seven Spirits—for they are said to be before the
throne. Therefore you could not identify them with the
Father or the Lamb.

—from (2) and (4) and (6) *the mysterious union* betwixt God
and them—for they are called the eyes of Jehovah; the
spirits whom the Son of man hath—the eyes of the Lamb.

Father and the Lord Jesus, so is there likewise betwixt them and the seven-fold Spirit of God.

In this stage of our inquiry it will be enough to ask ourselves, In the cases cited above, was the co-operating Spirit identical with the Father or with the Son? Could you say it was the Father or the Son who descended on Christ at his baptism, or on the apostles at Pentecost? Could you assert that we are baptized into the name of the Father, and of the Son, and of one who likewise is the Father, or the Son? Or that grace and peace are besought from the eternal Father, and from one who under another name is also the Father, and from Jesus Christ? No one could maintain this for a moment. The Holy Ghost, therefore, cannot be identified or confounded either with the eternal Father, or with his Son Jesus Christ our Lord.

(2) I proceed, then, to consider, that such personal properties and actions are ascribed to the Spirit as prove independent and intelligent personality.

But, it is asked, do we not read of the Spirit of God

—from (3) again, that they denote a willing intelligence and not an abstract power—for to imagine that John prays to seven abstractions in parity with the Father and the Son for grace and peace is inconceivable.

That they cannot be angels is manifest, for the worshipping of angels is expressly forbidden.

Col. ii. 18.

Comparing, therefore, the other passages with (1)—remembering how Jesus Christ says that the Scripture, "The Spirit of the Lord God is upon me" was fulfilled in himself—and knowing that "in the Oriental style the perfection of any quality is expressed by the number seven,"—we may fairly conclude this expression represents to us "this heavenly Agent, the Holy Ghost, in his own original and infinite perfection, in the consummate wisdom of his operations, and in the gracious munificence of his gifts."

Isai. lxi. 1.
Luke iv. 21.

Pye Smith

being "poured out," and "given in greater or less degree?" If he were a Person, how could he be thus effused or divided? Here we fully admit that the terms "spirit" and "holy spirit," do *sometimes* denote not the person, but the operations, the gifts, the influences of the Holy Ghost: as, for example, when it is said, "I will take of the spirit which is upon thee." ^{Num. xi. 17.} But the question is not whether some passages may not be brought forward which denote the operations and influences of the Spirit, and therefore do *not* establish the point; but whether besides these there are not very numerous portions of Scripture which *do* positively and unanswerably establish his personality. Just as if I were studying a work on horticulture, and because the writer here and there used the term "sun" to denote the influences of the sun, directing me to place certain plants *in the sun*, or that *more or less sun* should be admitted, I were to contend, that the author could not believe there was actually such a globe of light in the heavens, although in many other parts he had spoken in strictly astronomical language of our planetary system. You would justly assure me, that the occasional recurrence of such familiar phrases as "more or less sun, etc." was no valid argument against his conviction of the sun's real existence, stated elsewhere in the volume plainly and positively. Now, we admit, that by "the spirit," are sometimes intended the gifts and graces of the Spirit. These graces may be poured out—these gifts distributed. But "all these worketh that one and the self-same Spirit, dividing to every man severally as he will."*   1 Cor. xii. 11.

---

* The substance of the above paragraph is taken from a valuable sermon of the Rev. J. E. Bates, "On the Holy Spirit."

Now if, altogether apart from this investigation, you had been asked to name those qualities which evidence personal existence, you would have been quite content to answer: Show me that which has mind, and affection, and will, which can act, and speak, and direct; and that sentient, loving, determining agent, speaker, and ruler, must possess personality, or personality cannot exist.

But we read in Scripture of—

The mind of the Spirit. "He that searcheth the hearts knoweth what is the mind (or intention) of the Spirit, because he maketh intercession." Rom. viii. 27.

The infinite comprehension of the Spirit. "The things of God knoweth no one, but the Spirit of God." See next section, where this passage is referred to more at length. 1 Cor. ii. 11.

The fore-knowledge of the Spirit. "He will show you things to come." John xvi. 13.

The power of the Spirit. "That ye may abound in hope through the power of the Holy Ghost." If the Spirit were a metonymy for the power of God, this would be a most unlikely combination. Rom. xv. 13.

The love of the Spirit. "I beseech you for the love of the Spirit" (διὰ τῆς ἀγάπης τοῦ Πνεύματος):—a plea exactly corresponding with one he had used shortly before. "I beseech you, by the mercies of God" (διὰ τῶν οἰκτιρμῶν τοῦ Θεοῦ.) Rom. xv. 30. Rom. xii. 1.

The self-determining will of the Spirit. "Dividing to every man severally as he will." 1 Cor. xii. 11.

We find—

He creates and gives life. "The Spirit of God hath made me, and the breath of the Almighty hath given me life." And again, "By the word of the Lord were the heavens made; and all the host of them by the breath (Spirit) of his mouth." Job xxxiii. 4. Psa. xxxiii. 6.

He strives with the ungodly. "My Spirit shall not always strive with man." Gen. vi. 3.

He convinces of sin, righteousness, and judgment. John xvi. 8.

He new-creates the soul. "Born of the Spirit." John iii. 5—8.

He commands and forbids. "The Spirit said to Philip, "Go near.—The Spirit bade me go with them. Acts viii. 29. Acts xi. 12.—The Holy Ghost said, Separate me Barnabas and Acts xiii. 2. Saul.—Being forbidden by the Holy Ghost to preach. Acts xvi. 6, 7.—The Spirit suffered them not."

He appoints ministers in the church. "The flock over which the Holy Ghost hath made you overseers." Acts xx. 28.

He inspired the sacred writers. "Holy men spake as they were moved by the Holy Ghost." 2 Pet. i. 21.

He speaketh expressly of events "in the latter times." 1 Tim. iv. 1.

He saith to the churches the messages of the S of man. Rev. ii. 7, etc.

He performs miracles. "Then the Spirit took me up, and I heard behind me a voice—The Spirit lifted me Ezek. iii. 12. up, between the earth and the heaven. The Spirit Ezek. viii. 3. gave them utterance [at Pentecost]. The Spirit of the Acts ii. 4. Lord caught away Philip. Mighty signs and wonders Acts viii. 39. (were done) by the power of the Spirit of God." Rom. xv. 19.

He caused the virgin Mary to conceive. Luke i. 95.

He works in all saints, dispensing divers gifts with independent spontaneity of choice. 1 Cor. xii. 4–11.

He regenerates and seals his people, for we are saved by his renewing;—and are "sealed unto the day of Tit. iii. 5. redemption" by the Holy Spirit of God. Eph. iv. 30.

He intercedes for us in prayers, for he "helpeth our infirmities....and maketh intercession for us." Rom. viii. 26.

He teaches and comforts and guides us into all truth. For Christ promises, "The Comforter, which is the Holy Ghost, whom the Father will send in my name, He (ἐκεῖνος) shall teach you all things—shall testify John xiv. 26. of me—shall guide you into all truth—shall glorify me—and shall take of mine, and show it unto you." John xvi. 13, 14.

He can be vexed and grieved. "They returned and vexed his Holy Spirit." "Grieve not the Holy Spirit of God."

Isai. lxiii. 10.
Eph. iv. 30.

He is designated by the use of masculine pronouns, though the noun itself, Spirit, is neuter. "When he, the Spirit (ἐκεῖνος,τὸ Πνεῦμα) of truth, is come, he will guide you," and so continually in this context, where it might be rendered "That person the Spirit." Thus, likewise: "That Holy Spirit of promise, who (ὅς) is the earnest of our inheritance."

John xvi. 13.

Eph. i. 13, 14.

He testifies with personal witnesses. "He shall testify (μαρτυρεῖτε) and ye also testify (μαρτυρήσει), —"We are his witnesses of these things; and so is also the Holy Ghost."

John xv. 26, 27.

Acts v. 32.

He approves with personal counsellors. "It seemed good to the Holy Ghost, and to us."

Acts xv. 28.

He invites with personal messengers. "The Spirit and the bride say, Come."

Rev. xxii. 17.

He is personally present in a sense in which Jesus is personally absent. "It is expedient for you that I go away; for if I go not away, the Comforter will not come unto you."

John xvi. 7.

He can be personally blasphemed (as Christ may be personally blasphemed), *but only upon peril of eternal condemnation.* "Whosoever speaketh a word against the Son of man, it shall be forgiven him; but whosoever speaketh against the Holy Ghost, it shall not be forgiven him, neither in this world, neither in the world to come."

Matt. xii. 32.

Gal. iv. 6.

He cries in our hearts, "Abba, Father."

He repeats the beatitude pronounced on those who sleep in Jesus. "Yea, saith the Spirit, that they may rest from their labours."

Rev. xiv. 13.

Surely, from a calm and comprehensive study of this

testimony, we must conclude that if these qualities
and actions do not prove personality, there are none,
however explicit and exact, which can do so. Unitarians are wont to speak of the Spirit, as an effusion or
emanation separate from God, or an influence or power
exercised by God. Can you speak of the mind of an
effusion?—of an emanation, knowing the depths of
him from whom it distils?—of an influence, or power,
or aught impersonal, revealing future events; possessing a power, and love, and will of its own; cre-
ating, striving, convincing, recreating; enjoining,
prohibiting, commissioning; inspiring, speaking expressly, addressing the church; performing miracles,
transporting, giving utterance; energizing, regenerat-
ing, sealing; interceding, teaching, comforting, guid-
ing; being vexed and grieved; testifying, approving,
inviting; being present as a personal Comforter who
may be personally blasphemed, crying in us until he ^{Cf. Gal. iv. 6;}
teaches us to cry, Abba, Father, and repeating on
earth the heaven-sent benediction on departed saints?
If in some few instances you might thus personify an
influence, most of those adduced, taken singly, resist
such an interpretation; and taken collectively, would,
if thus understood, confuse all the laws of language,
and thus derange the first principles of truth.

It is not easy to translate into our own tongue the
proof we obtain from a study of the original here. But
suppose in a volume of history you met with the following passage:—"The prince having left this province
thought good that his Majesty's power should occupy
his room: as for this power, he knew the secret counsels of the king; he had an independent will; he
strove with the ill-affected, and was grieved and vexed
with the obstinacy of some, while others he convinced
of their infatuation, and was enabled to train as good

citizens; he consoled the well-disposed; he issued commands and restrictions at his own pleasure; he appointed subordinate officers; he spoke expressly of the certain issue of some incipient plots; he accomplished prodigies of benevolence: indeed such was the authority of this power, that whoever wilfully insulted him was by the king's command imprisoned for life; while on the other hand, he was accustomed to repeat assurances which came direct from court, of the favour awarded there to faithful subjects." Would you, could you doubt for a moment whether or not this power was a personal intelligent agent? And if, a few pages further on in the book, you read, "And thus his Majesty's power was extended and his dominion consolidated," would you because of the repetition of the term *power*, or *his Majesty's power*, confuse the latter abstraction with the former person—would you gainsay your previous unhesitating conclusion, that the power left in that province was a living person? It is impossible. You would say, honest language, though capable of metaphor, is incapable of such delusive impersonations. So likewise the witness of Scripture, which we have heard, is unequivocal that the Holy Spirit is a living Agent working with consciousness, will, and love.

(3) Now to this agent Divine attributes are ascribed, and by him Divine offices are exercised towards us.

He is eternal. "Christ through the eternal (αἰωνίου) Spirit offered himself." This is the same word which is used of the self-existence from everlasting to everlasting of Jehovah.

He is omnipresent. "Whither shall I go from thy Spirit? Or whither shall I flee from thy presence? If I ascend up into heaven thou art there." Having proved his distinct personality, this establishes his om-

Heb. ix. 14.

Rom. xvi. 26.

Psa. cxxxix. 7, 8.

nipresence: which truth is indeed self-evident, from
the simultaneous work he is carrying on in ten thousand hearts throughout the universe.

He is omniscient. For he alone, with the infinite
Son, comprehends the incomprehensible Jehovah.
"God hath revealed them to us by his Spirit: for
the Spirit searcheth all things, even the deep things of
God. For what man knoweth the things of man,
save the spirit of man which is in him? Even so, the
things of God knoweth no one but the Spirit of God." 1 Cor. ii. 10, 11.
The word *search*, as used in Scripture, does not neces-
sarily imply that successive acquisition of knowledge
which belongs to a finite being, for Jehovah says, "I
the Lord, search the heart." "And that the Spirit Jer. xvii. 10.
here is not a mere quality of Divine nature, as consciousness is of the human mind, appears from the
first clause, 'God hath revealed them to us by his
Spirit,' which clearly implies a personal distinction;
for it could not be said that a man makes anything
known to others by his consciousness." P. Smith Appendix II.

He is prescient and unveils futurity. "It was revealed unto him (Simeon) by the Holy Ghost that he
should not see death before he had seen the Lord's Luke ii. 26.
Christ." "He will show you things to come." And John xvi. 13.
John "was in the Spirit" when he was enabled to Rev. i. 10; iv. 1, 2.
cast his eye across the chart of providence.

He is absolutely free and independent. "The wind
bloweth where it listeth—so is every one that is born John iii. 8.
of the Spirit." Dividing as he willeth. "Where the 1 Cor. xii. 11.
Spirit of the Lord is, there is liberty." 2 Cor. iii. 17.

He is infinitely good and holy. "Thou gavest thy
good Spirit to instruct them." "Thy Spirit is good." Neh. ix. 20. Psa. cxliii. 10.
He is called in the Old Testament, emphatically, the
Holy Spirit of God. He is repeatedly styled by our Psa. li. 11. Isai. lxiii. 10, 11.
Lord, the Holy Spirit. And this is his distinctive Luke xi. 13.

designation by the apostles throughout the New Testa-

John xiv. 17,
etc. ment. He is likewise called "the Spirit of truth, and

John xiv. 17.
Rom. i. 4. the Spirit of holiness," as the fountain of verity and
goodness.

He is the Almighty Creator of all things. Here it
may suffice to quote one passage which may well set
the question at rest for ever. "Who hath measured
the waters in the hollow of his hand, and meted out
heaven with a span, and comprehended the dust of the
earth in a measure, and weighed the mountains in
scales, and the hills in a balance? Who hath directed
the Spirit of the Lord, or being his counsellor hath
taught him? With whom took he counsel, and who
Isai. xl. 12–14. instructed him?" No words could express more
plainly an intelligent Creator, inferior to none, whose
wisdom was his own, whose counsel was underived,
whose omnipotence was inherent. What reflex light
this casts on the simple declaration of Genesis, "The
Gen. i. 2. Spirit of God moved on the face of the waters!"

In his hands are the issues of life and death. "The
Job xxxi.i. 4. Spirit of God hath made me.—Thou sendest forth thy
Psa. civ. 30. Spirit: they are created.—The grass withereth, the
flower fadeth: because the Spirit of the Lord bloweth
Isai. xl. 7. upon it: surely the people is grass."

And then, as to the life of God within us, he is *the
author and finisher* of it. He begets and quickens the
John iii. 6. soul, once dead in trespasses and sins. He teaches us
Rom. viii. 26.
1 Cor. iii. 16. to pray. He dwells in us, as in his temple. He pro-
Gal. v. 22, 23. duces his own celestial fruits. He sheds abroad the
love of God in our hearts. He seals us unto the day
Eph. iv. 30. of redemption. He works in us, educates us, comforts
us, leads us, and bears witness with our spirit that we
Rom. viii. 9—
16. are the children of God. He carries on the work of
sanctification, changes us into the Divine image from
2 Cor. iii. 18. glory to glory. And by him, as the One who quick-

ened Christ our Head, will God quicken our mortal
bodies at the last day.

Now I venture to ask, as I asked respecting the
testimony of Jesus, who can believe those explicit declarations of the character and work of the Holy Spirit,
and not repose their whole confidence in him—resting
on him with supreme reliance, and loving him with
entire devotion? Consider, he is eternal, everywhere
present, infinite in wisdom, prescient, absolutely just,
and is perfect in goodness and grace and truth! Consider, further, so close and necessary is our relationship
to him, that he is the Almighty Creator of that world
in which we live; that he gives us every breath we
draw, and that he suspends that breath when we die.
Consider, the whole work of the spiritual life within
us, from its earliest germ to its latest development, is
his operation. What frail and finite creature, like
man, believing this testimony, could, in the presence
of such an One, refuse to render him adoring trust
and love? If Scripture forbade these emotions, as due
only to Deity, we should be rent in twain. But does
Scripture forbid them? Nay, verily. You cannot
find the faintest hint against depending on the Holy
Spirit too absolutely. There is no jealousy of his
claims. The most humble submission to his education
is ever enforced; any violation of reverent regard is Eph. iv. 30.
deprecated with a plaintive earnestness of expostual- 1 Thess. v. 19.
tion; and wilful blasphemy against him is fenced with
the most awful warning in the whole word of God.
Such is the efficacy of his personal presence, that it is
represented as compensating the personal absence of
Jesus. Every affectionate and trustful desire is
awakened in you; for in the comfort he imparts, as
explained by Christ, is comprised the communication
of every Divine blessing. The claims of no benefactor

can transcend those of him who gives us life and light, emancipating us from the thraldom of sin, and bringing us into the freedom of love. Only believe these Scriptures, and you must, perforce, trust and love this Divine Spirit supremely. This homage belongs to God alone, whose name is Jealous, who will not give his glory to another. Therefore we conclude and confess that the Holy Ghost is one with God, and is himself God, himself Jehovah.

(4) This is further established by the fact that the Spirit of God is revealed in Scripture as the object of religious worship in parity with the Father and the Son.

The sixth chapter of Isaiah compared with John xii. 41, has already proved to us that God manifested himself to the prophet by the express image of his person, his only begotten Son. The voice which spoke is distinctly said to be the voice of Jehovah. But the message then sent is again recorded by Paul, and is prefaced with this remarkable introduction: "Well, spake the Holy Ghost by Esaias the prophet?" The glory of Jehovah of hosts was then revealed by Jesus Christ, and the voice of Jehovah was the utterancè of the Holy Ghost. Now we decipher the true significance of the threefold adoration of the veiled seraphim, "Holy, holy, holy, Lord of hosts," and dimly apprehend why it was asked, "Who will go for *us*." The angels of light, therefore, worship the Holy Spirit with the Father and the Son.

I would mention in passing, without laying stress upon it, the impressive vision of Ezekiel, in the valley of dry bones, in which he is commanded to address the wind ($\pi\nu\varepsilon\tilde{u}\mu\alpha$—*LXX*), "Prophesy unto the wind, prophesy, Son of man, and say to the wind, Thus saith

Isai. vi. 8.

Acts xxviii. 25.

Isai. vi. 3; ver. 8.

the Lord God: Come from the four winds, O breath, and breathe upon these slain, that they may live." The Ezek. xxxvii. 9. wind is evidently typical of the Spirit, for it is said in the interpretation of the vision, "I will put my Spirit in you, and ye shall live:" and to my own mind the ver. 14. proclamation to the wind is typical of prayer to the Spirit for his energizing power in quickening dead Compare chap. xxxvi. 27, with 37. souls to the life of God.

The baptismal formulary, however, affords an unambiguous testimony. For "baptism is a solemn act of worship, denoting entire consecration to him in whose name we are baptized. It is the stipulation (ἐπερώτημα 1 Pet. iii. 21. Greek legal term) of a good conscience toward God. Now the existence of a stipulation implies the presence, or in some way the knowledge and acceptance, of the person to whom the engagement is made. It supposes then, in this case, the presence or cognizance of the Son and the Spirit equally with that of the Father." Pye Smith. Here again we have, by our Lord's express command, adoring homage paid to the Holy Ghost in union with the Father and himself, at this sacred profession of every Christian's faith.

I would also ask you to compare—

O come, let us worship and bow down: let us kneel before the Lord our Maker. For he is the Lord our God; and we are the people of his pasture, and the sheep of his hand. To-day, if ye will hear his voice, harden not your hearts, as in the provocation, and as in the day of temptation in the wilderness: when your fathers tempted me, proved me, and saw my works. —Psa. xcv. 6—9.

Wherefore, as the Holy Ghost saith, To-day, if ye will hear his voice, harden not your hearts, as in the provocation, in the day of temptation in the wilderness, when your fathers tempted me. —Heb. iii. 7—9.

They vexed his Holy Spirit. —Isai. lxiii. 10.

Your fathers resisted the Holy Ghost.—Acts vii. 51.

[The context in the last two shows it refers to the provocation in the wilderness.]

We may fairly conclude that the One whom the psalmist calls upon us to worship is the same One whom, he says, the Israelites provoked. This One the parallel passages assure us was eminently the Eternal Spirit. I say eminently, for I do not think these and other like Scriptures warrant us in excluding thoughts of the Father and the Son. While establishing the personal Deity of the Spirit, we must not forget his essential unity with the Father and the Son. To those who believe this, every simple command "worship God" embraces the worship of the Holy Spirit; but in the above it was *eminently* the Spirit. The Spirit was the One of the sacred Trinity most prominently tempted and grieved by the Israelites, and therefore the One most prominently to be supplicated.*

---

* Since the above was written I have found the following passages in the Life of Thomas Scott the commentator, which present in a condensed form the arguments for the truth which I am here endeavouring to advocate.

"The form of blessing, *into the name of the Father, and of the Son, and of the Holy Ghost*, seems to me to recognize God our Saviour as Father, Son, and Holy Ghost. In this view, when God is addressed without personal distinction, I consider the address as made to the God of salvation; and the Holy Spirit *included* whether prayer or praise be offered. The *trishagion* or threefold ascription of holiness to *Jehovah* both in the Old and New Testament, seems an act of worship to the Holy Spirit together with the Father and the Son. The form of blessing appointed by Moses, in this view, implies a prayer to the Holy Spirit, Numb. vi. 24—27; as does the apostolical benediction, 2 Cor. xiii. 14. I have no hesitation in my mind as to the express act of adoration, in Rev. i. 4, being offered personally to the Holy Spirit, according to the emblematical language of that book..... If, then, we be fully convinced that the Holy Spirit is God, and that all Divine perfections and operations, together with every personal property, are ascribed to him, there can be no doubt but he is the object of Divine adoration. Where God is addressed

Pray ye, therefore, the Lord of the harvest that he will thrust forth labourers into his harvest. —*Matt.* ix. 38.

The Holy Ghost said, Separate me Barnabas and Saul for the work. So they, being sent forth by the Holy Ghost.—*Acts* xiii. 2—4.

Here Christ himself enjoins prayer to him, who sends forth ministers. That this is one special office of the Holy Ghost, we learn from the Acts; and we have, therefore, Christ's warrant for praying to the Spirit.

Again, bearing in mind that "the love of God is shed abroad in our hearts by the Holy Ghost," this being his peculiar office, I pray you to ponder the following prayers: ^{Rom. v. 5.}

"The Lord make you to increase and abound in love one toward another, and toward all men, even as we do toward you: to the end he may establish your hearts unblamable in holiness before God, even our Father, at the coming of our Lord Jesus Christ."—1 *Thess.* iii. 12, 13.

"The Lord direct your hearts into the love of God, and into the patient waiting for Christ."—2 *Thess.* iii. 5.

In both these supplications we have the Father and Christ named besides the One to whom the prayer is addressed; may we not be assured that this One is especially the blessed Spirit of love?

The Book of Revelation seals the testimony. For, as we have seen, the bestowal of grace and peace is implored equally from the eternal Father, and from the seven Spirits which are before his throne, and from Jesus Christ. This is direct supplication. And lastly, ^{Rev. i. 4, 5,}

without distinction of persons, the Holy Spirit is virtually addressed: all that dependence, gratitude, love and honour, which are required as due to our God, are required towards the Holy Spirit; and therefore worship and adoring praise and prayer cannot be improper." Life of Scott, pp. 338, 339.

we have in the fourth and fifth chapters a view, couched in symbolic but most expressive language, of the celestial worship. A throne is set in heaven. It is then a question of absorbing interest who is the adorable Being, who there concentrates around himself this homage of saints and angels. So singular and sublime a revelation must needs draw the closest regards of every reverent mind; for though "the secret things belong to the Lord our God," the "things which Deut. xxix. 29. are revealed belong to us and to our children." Is then the unity of the One there worshipped so simple an unity as to preclude any plurality subsisting therein? The throne was set in heaven, and One sat on the throne. But is this One alone in infinite solitariness? The Lord enable us to keep our foot as we draw near to his unutterable glory. What saith the Scripture? The voice of the Son of man was only now silent. "I overcame, and am set down with my Rev. iii. 21. Father in his throne." (An evident distinction is here drawn betwixt the throne of Christ, which his people were admitted to share, and the throne of the Father, the supreme glories of which the son alone partakes.) And in strict accordance with this we find, "Lo, in the midst of the throne*. . . . . . stood a Lamb as it Rev. v. 6. had been slain:" and the universal worship of heaven

---

* If any object that, in chap. iv. 6, it is said, "the living creatures were in the midst of the throne, and round about the throne." I believe the answer is given in the parallel vision of Ezekiel i. 5, 22, 26, where the throne is on the firmament, and the firmament rests on the heads of the living creatures; "so that to one approaching the throne they would seem to be around it, though their bodies were *under* or 'in the midst' of it as a support."— Barnes. That they did not occupy the throne and receive adoration is plain; for (chap. v. 6) the Lamb appears in the midst of the living creatures, as well as in the midst of the elders; and ver. 8, they, with the elders, fall down before him.

is addressed equally "to him that sat on the throne
and unto the Lamb for ever." But is this all? Have
we now reached the limit of that revealed? I think
not. The question must press on every reflective student, what position do the "seven Spirits of God"
hold amid this tide of celestial adoration? Are they
among the worshippers, or are they worshipped? In
the benediction of the first chapter they mysteriously
intervene betwixt the Father and the Son, as one of
the blessed Three who are the fountain of grace and
peace. In the third chapter the Son of man describes
himself as having the seven Spirits of God. In the
fourth chapter they appear as seven lamps of fire
burning before the throne. But what when next we
read of them? "In the midst of the throne, and of
the four living creatures, and in the midst of the elders,
stood a Lamb as it had been slain,* having seven horns Rev. v. 6.
and seven eyes, which are the seven Spirits of God
sent forth into all the earth." This implies their
closest union with the Lamb; therefore, when he, together with the eternal Father, received that wondrous
universal homage, the sevenfold Spirit of God must
have received it with him. How beautiful now appears the harmony with the opening benedictory
prayer! and how appropriate now the threefold
cherubic adoration, "Holy, holy, holy, Lord God Al-

---

* If one passing mention only had been made of them, as of the
seven horns, we might have said these shadowed forth perfect
knowledge, as those perfect power: but the repeated and varied
way, in which they are introduced, prevents our resting in this
abstract interpretation; and hence the conjunction of the seven
horns in this verse seems equivalent to such expressions as "Jesus
returned in the power of the Spirit (the same personal Spirit who
had descended on him at his baptism, and led him into the wil- Luke iv. 14.
derness) into Galilee:" or, "God anointed Jesus of Nazareth with Luke iii. 22;
the Holy Ghost and with power." iv. 1.
Acts x. 38.

mighty, which was, and is, and is to come!" The vision is symbolic, but it symbolizes truth; and it is most suggestive of the highest adoration being received on the eternal throne by the Father, and by the Son, and by the Holy Ghost.

Divine worship is, therefore, on the authority of Scripture, rendered to the Spirit. I admit that in some of the cases the evidence is rather circumstantial than direct. But this we should have *a priori* expected; for in the economy of redemption it is the office of the Holy Ghost to kindle in us "the spirit of grace and of supplications," to intercede for us and with us, and to enable us, in the spirit of adoption, to pray as Jesus taught his disciples, "Our Father which art in heaven."

Zech. xii. 10.

Rom. viii. 15, 26, 27.

(5) Finally, the comparison of Scripture with Scripture demonstrates that the Divine Spirit* is Jehovah and God.

Cf. Serle and Jones.

| And the Lord said, My Spirit shall not always strive with man.—*Gen.* vi. 3. | The long-suffering of God waited in the days of Noah.—1 *Pet.* iii. 20. |

It was then the forbearance of God the Spirit with which they before the flood contended.

| They vexed his Holy Spirit... Where is he that put his Holy Spirit within him?....that led them through the deep.....The Spirit of Jehovah caused him to rest.—*Isai.* lxiii. 10—14. | Jehovah said to Moses, How long will this people provoke me.—*Numb.* xiv. 11. Jehovah alone did lead him. —*Deut.* xxxii. 12. |

Compare also the parallel passages (p. 125). Here we learn that the One provoked was the Holy Spirit, and was Jehovah. Therefore the Spirit is Jehovah.

---

* This appellative is not modern. Thrice, at least, is the Hebrew "Spirit of God" rendered by the *L X X.* (Πνεῦμα Θεῖον)—*Exod.* xxxi. 3; *Job.* xxvii. 3; xxxiii. 4.

The Spirit of the Lord spake by me; and his word was in my tongue.—2 *Sam.* xxiii. 2.	The God of Israel said, the Rock of Israel spake to me.—2 *Sam.* xxiii. 3.

Therefore, unless you admit that there were three, or at least two, Divine speakers who inspired David, the Spirit of Jehovah is the God and the Rock of Israel.

Well spake the Holy Ghost by Esaias the Prophet.—*Acts* xxviii. 25.	The Lord God of Israel.... spake by the mouth of his holy prophets, which have been since the world began.—*Luke* i. 68–70.
Holy men of God spake as they were moved by the Holy Ghost.—2 *Pet.* i.,21.	All Scripture is given by inspiration of God.—2 *Tim.* iii. 16.

The Spirit, therefore, is God, yea, the Lord God of Israel. I append a few other passages, (selected from many,) the conclusion from which is similarly self-evident.

That which is born of the Spirit (τὸ γεγεννημένον ἐχ τοῦ Πνεύματος).—*John* iii. 6.	That which is born of God τὸ γεγεννημένον ἐχ τοῦ Θεοῦ)—1 *John* v. 4.
Christ wrought by me, through mighty signs and wonders by the power of the Holy Ghost.—*Rom.* xviii; 19.	Jehovah,.......the Lord of lords....the God of gods,.... alone doeth great wonders.—*Ps.* cxxxvi. 1—4.
TheComforter (ὁ Παράχλητος) which is the Holy Ghost.—*John* xiv. 26.	I, even I, am he that comforteth (ὁ παραχαλῶν)—*L X X.*) you.—*Isai.* li. 12.
Walking . . in the comfort of the Holy Ghost.—*Acts* ix. 31.	The God of all comfort, who comforteth us.—2 *Cor.* i. 3, 4.
Why hath Satan filled thine heart to lie to the Holy Ghost? —*Acts* v. 3.	Thou hast not lied unto men, but unto God.—*Acts* v. 4.
How is it that ye have agreed to tempt the Spirit of the Lord? —*Acts* v. 9.	Thou shalt not tempt the Lord thy God.—*Matt.* iv. 7.
Your body is the temple of the Holy Ghost.—1 *Cor.* vi. 19. The Spirit of God dwelleth in you.—1 *Cor.* iii. 16.	Ye are the temple of the living God; as God has said, I will dwell in them.—2 *Cor.* vi. 16.

These passages might be greatly multiplied; but from this comparison, observing the way in which the names and offices of God and of the Holy Spirit are interchanged, we conclude that this same Eternal Spirit is Jehovah, the God of Israel, the Lord God, the Lord of lords, the God of gods, the living God, the Divine Being who quickens and comforts—in one word, he is God.* Once more, Paul affirms, "We are changed into the same image, AS BY THE LORD THE SPIRIT" (καθάπερ ἀπὸ Κυρίου πνεύματος). The Greek should, doubtless, be thus rendered: for construction, compare Gal. i. 3 (ἀπὸ Θεοῦ πατρός). He thus places the word LORD, which he had used, ver. 16, to designate Jehovah, in direct and immediate apposition with SPIRIT. The whole context, which so beautifully illustrates the threefold work of the Holy Trinity in the believer's soul, proves, at the same time, that the Holy Ghost is one with the Father and the Son,—very and Eternal God.

2 Cor. iii. 18.

If any object that he is said to be sent by the Father and the Son, and that this mission implies inferiority, we answer that, even among men, the being sent is by no means always a mark of subordination. "The members of a senate consult together relative to some nego-

---

* I might here add two remarks:

(1) The Deity of Christ being proved, the very fact of the Holy Spirit anointing this infinite Saviour for all the work of redemption proves his own Divine Infinitude;—for who but God could empower God?

(2) As in the Old Testament we find Christ as the Angel of God's presence saying, "I am the God of thy father,—I will send thee;" thus claiming supreme authority; and as from thence we may securely infer the Deity of this glorious leader; so in the New Testament, when we find the Spirit said to Peter, "Arise, go, for I have sent them," thus, in his own right, setting aside the ceremonial law, we may safely argue, this is a Divine person ,who, in the absence of the Son of God, according to his promise, acts in his place and governs his church.

Ex. iii. 6, 10.

Acts x. 19, 20.

tiation, in executing which great wisdom, judgment, and experience are required. It is resolved to send one of their number. Is it any mark of inferiority to be selected, and sent on such a service? And the mission of the Comforter is spoken of regarding the office he has undertaken in the economy of grace—the work of sanctifying the elect people of God—a work which none less than God can effect, and the glorious accomplishment of which will redound to his praise through the countless ages of eternity." Bates.

If, again, any ask why the ambiguity inseparable from the name *Spirit of God*, when compared with the phrase *spirit of a man*—an ambiguity which, unless explained, would have tended to conceal his personality —was permitted; I would suggest that his name is no arbitrary choice; that it is the only one which would reveal to us the distinctive character of this holy Being, as the name *the Son* could alone describe the Eternal Word; and that the very similarity of designation may be needful to express his fellowship with us, his spiritual indwelling, and the high communion carried on, while the Spirit itself bears witness with our spirit that we are the children of God. This Rom. viii. 16. similarity testifies to us our union with the Divine Comforter who renews us, as our common humanity testifies our union with the Divine Saviour who redeemed us.

And if once more it is asked, why he is not more prominently set forth in Scripture as the object of adoration, besides the answer given above, there seems in this, if I may venture so to express myself, a principle of Divine equipoise in the parts sustained in our salvation, by the co-equal and co-eternal Three. The love of the Father, loving us so that he gave his Son to redeem and his Spirit to sanctify us, shines preeminent: it bathes the sacred page with light, and commands our homage, and compels our love. The grace of the Lord Jesus, for us incarnate, for us crucified, for us interceding, absorbs every thought, and attracts every affection: and a large portion of Scripture is taken up with setting forth the eternal Deity of Emmanuel, and requiring us to regard him with equal love and with equal confidence. Once more, a third is revealed, the Divine Comforter: the glories of his Person are beyond doubt affirmed, but they are only rarely disclosed in full view; his worship is enjoined, but it is comparatively withdrawn from observation: when, however, we look into the subjective work carried on by him, there is an amplitude and plenitude of evidence from Holy Writ, which entirely compensates any seclusion of his visible majesty. The variety of his Divine operations in us as far exceeds in glory, as the brightness of his presence is concealed. The ministration of the Spirit is as mighty, as his voice is mysteriously still.

But here, even when we would feel our way with the utmost reverence, how soon are we beyond our depth! The waters are risen, waters to swim in, a river that cannot be passed over. Thanks be to God, the necessary truth is clear as the light:—that the Holy Spirit is distinct from the Father and the Son; that such personal properties are assigned to him as demonstrate intelligent personality; that all Divine attributes, such as self-existence from eternity, omnipresence, infinite wisdom and foreknowledge, absolute freedom and goodness, creative providential and spiritual power —attributes any one of which would prove his Deity—are assigned to him; that he is associated in Divine offices with the Father and the Son; that he with them is worshipped and glorified; that he is

Ezek. xlvi. 5.

Jehovah and God:—these things are written, as with
a sun-beam, in the Scriptures of truth.

But here I would remind myself and my readers
that no evidence, however conclusive, can insure a
saving belief in the Divinity of the Holy Ghost. The
understanding may be convinced, while the heart may
rebel. For the Lord Jesus says to his disciples, "I
will pray the Father, and he shall give you another
Comforter, that he may abide with you for ever; even
the Spirit of truth; whom the world cannot receive,
because it seeth him not, neither knoweth him." And John xiv. 16, 17.
the apostle Paul, while in conscious integrity he declares, We speak the things freely given to us of
God, "not in the words which man's wisdom teacheth,
but which the Holy Ghost teacheth; comparing spirit-
ual things with spiritual," seems to chasten his hopes 1 Cor. ii. 12, 13.
with the humbling recollection, "the natural man
receiveth not the things of the Spirit of God, .. neither
can he know them, because they are spiritually dis- ver. 14
cerned." And therefore rather, seeing we have a
High Priest who is touched with the feeling of our
infirmities, let us kneel together at the throne of grace,
and plead in prayer his own royal promise, "If ye
then, being evil, know how to give good gifts unto your
children, how much more shall your heavenly Father
give the Holy Spirit to them that ask him!"—that we Luke xi. 13.
all, with open face beholding as in a glass the glory of
the Lord, may be changed into the same image from
glory to glory, as by the Lord the Spirit. 2 Cor. iii. 18.

CHAPTER VII

AND now I must seek to draw this treatise, which has extended far beyond the limits I designed, to a conclusion. I would therefore state my last proposition in these words:—

That Scripture, in the Old and the New Testament alike, assures us that in the trustful knowledge of One God,—the Father, the Son, and the Holy Ghost,—is the spiritual life of man now and for ever.

The Lord grant that we may continue to bring to the study of his word, that humble spirit which prays —"That which I see not teach thou me."

Job xxxiv. 32.

(1) **To** one who receives with meekness the engrafted word which is able to save our souls, the Scriptures already adduced prove beyond contradiction that as the Father is God, so is Jesus Christ God, and so the Holy Spirit is God. This truth, however, must be combined with another, which is revealed with equal clearness and enforced with equal solemnity:—"I am Jehovah, and there is none else, there is no God beside me." The combination of these truths establishes the doctrine of the Holy Trinity, for "these Three must together subsist in one infinite Divine essence, called Jehovah or God; and as this essence must be indivisible, each of them must possess not a part or portion of it, but the whole fulness or perfection of the essential Godhead forming, in an unity of nature, One Eternal Jehovah, and therefore revealed by a plural noun* as the Jehovah Elohim, which comprehends

Isaiah xlv. 5.

---

* The reader will observe, throughout this treatise, that I have given no prominence to the argument derivable from the plural form of Elohim, and to the yet more suggestive language used by

these Three; but with this solemn qualification, that the Jehovah Elohim is in truth but one Jehovah, a Triune God, Father, Son, and Holy Ghost." Adapted from Sellon, pp. 46, 47.

God, "Let us make man in our image, after our likeness," and again, "Who will go for us?" But I should be doing injustice to my own convictions if I did not state, that I believe this language was intended to foster when kindled, and to awaken when dormant, the persuasion that there subsisted a plurality in the essential unity of Jehovah. Thus far, I think, the following extracts from Dr. P. Smith's essay abundantly bear me out:— Gen. i. 26.
Isai. vi. 8.

"The most usual appellation of the Deity in the original Scriptures of the Old Testament is *Elohim,* which is constantly translated "God;" but it is the regular plural of *Eloah,* which also occurs, though much less frequently than in the plural form, and is always translated in the same manner.

"This plural appellative is generally put in agreement with singular verbs, pronouns, and adjectives, as in Gen. i. 1, *Elohim created:—creavit Dii;—les Dieux crea.* This is the ordinary construction through the whole Hebrew Bible.

"But sometimes the apposition is made with verbs, pronouns, and adjectives, in the *plural* number likewise, and sometimes singulars and plurals are put together in the same agreement: as Gen. xx. 13, God (plural) caused me to wander—*vagari me fecerunt Dii;—les Dieux m'ont fait egarer.* Deut. v. 26, heard the voice of the living God (plural)—audivit vocem *Decorum viventium;—Des Dieux vivans,* etc.

"To these may be added the similar expressions, though without the word Elohim:—

Psa. cxlix. 2, Israel shall rejoice in his Maker (plural)—*in Creatoribus suis—;de ses Createurs.*

Isai. liv. 5, For thy Maker (plural) is thy husband (plural).

Eccles. xii. 1, Remember thy Creator (plural).

"The fact which principally requires our attention, is the constant use of Elohim, to designate the one and only God. It is not a little remarkable that, in the sacred books of a people who were separated from all other nations for this express object, viz. that they should bear a public and continual protest against polytheism—the ordinary name and style of the only living and true God should be in a plural form. Did some strange and insuperable necessity lie in the way? Was the language so poor that it could furnish

This supreme mystery must transcend all the powers of human thought; and the question must recur again and again, What saith the Scripture? Our imaginations must be counted as the small dust of the balance. Thus do you conceive that the very names "the Father, the Son" imply a certain point in duration beyond which the Father inhabited eternity alone? Your conception cannot countervail the assertion of Scripture, that the goings-forth of the Saviour have been from everlasting; or the words of Christ himself, adopting the formula which declares the Divine self-existence from eternity to eternity, "I am the first and the last."

Micah v. 2.

Rev. i. 11.

The illustration, before adduced, of the sun, its beams of light, and its vital heat, may offer some faint resemblance of this great mystery; for the beams of light are generated by the central orb; and yet the sun could not have existed, so far as we know, for a moment without emitting its radiance, nor the radiance have existed without diffusing its warmth: so

---

no other term? Or, if so, could not the wisdom of inspiration have suggested a new appellative, and for ever abolish the hazardous word? None of these reasons existed. The language was rich and copious. Besides "that glorious and fearful name, Jehovah," the appropriated and unique style of the true God, there was the *singular* form "Eloah" of the very word in question.

Deut. vi. 4.

" 'Hear, O Israel, Jehovah, our Elohim, one Jehovah!' This sentence was proclaimed as a kind of oracular *effatum*,—a solemn and authoritative principle to the Israelites. Had it been intended to assert such a unity in the Divine nature, as is absolutely solitary, and exclusive of every modification of plurality, would not the expression of necessity have been this, 'Hear, O Israel, Jehovah, our Elohim, one Eloah?' But as the words actually stand, they appear to be in the most definite and expressive manner designed to convey the idea, that, *notwithstanding* a real plurality intimated in the form Elohim, Jehovah is still ONE."

that "one is not before another, but only in order and relation to one another." But no creature can ade- Beveridge on Art. I. quately image forth the Creator, who asks, "To whom then will ye liken God? or what likeness will ye compare unto him?" Isai. xl. 18.

Again, do you imagine that the name of him who is alone Jehovah, cannot comprehend a Trinity in Unity? Your imagination is as nothing in contradiction of the words of Christ revealing the one Divine name, as "the name of the Father, and of the Son, and of the Holy Ghost." Do you asseverate the impossibility of three subsistences in one eternal essence? Remember, I pray you, the words, "Canst thou find out the Almighty unto perfection?" What Job xi. 7. do we know of the essence of created things? The pure white light seems indissolubly one; an unscientific man would, without hesitation, pronounce it uniform, and would utterly deny any plurality subsisting in its transparent simplicity. The colours of the rainbow seem evidently manifold; and the same man might refuse to credit their unity. Science stoops to analyze light; and we are told that—

The prismatic spectrum consists in reality of three spectra of nearly equal length, each of uniform colour; superposed one upon another; and that the colours which the actual spectrum exhibits, arise from the mixture of the uniform colours of these three spectra superposed. The colours of these three elementary spectra, according to Sir David Brewster, are red, yellow, and blue. He shows that by a combination of these three, not only all the colours exhibited in the prismatic spectrum may be reproduced, but their combination also produces white light. He contends, therefore, that the white light of the sun consists, not Lardner's Museum. vol. vii. p. 78. of seven, but of three constituent lights.

The unlearned man then, in his incredulity, would have denied an established fact. The unity of that pure white light was not so simple as he affirmed. More constituents than one subsist in its ethereal essence. But has science now fathomed the mysteries of light? So far from it, we read:—

Light is now proved to consist in the waves of a subtle and elastic ether, which pervades all space, and serves to communicate every impulse, from one part of the universe to another, with a speed almost inconceivable. In this luminous ether, matter seems to emulate the subtlety of thought. Invisible, and yet the only means by which all things are made visible; impalpable, and yet nourishing all material objects into life and beauty; so elastic, that when touched at one point, swift glances of light tremble through the universe; and still so subtle that the celestial bodies traverse its depths freely, and even the most vaporous comet scarcely exhibits a sensible retardation in its course:— there is something in the very nature of this medium which seems to baffle the powers of human science, and to say to the pride of human intellect, "Hitherto shalt thou come, but no further; and here shall thy proud waves be stayed." Here, indeed, the most brilliant and profound analysts have continually to guess their way, when they would trace out a few of the simplest laws resulting from the existence of such an ether, and unfold their application to the various phenomena of reflected and refracted light. It is a great deep of mystery. Science grows dizzy on its verge when it strives to explore the nature of this subtle, immense, imponderable ocean, which bathes all worlds in light, and itself remains, by its own nature, invisible for ever.

Birks'
Treasures
of Wisdom,
pp. 99—106.

Is such the modest confession of truth after all the triumphs of human wisdom? Is man only wading, with tremulous footstep, into the shallow waters of that unfathomable sea called into existence by the fiat of God, when he said, "Let there be light, and there was light?" Are we so soon out of our depth in seeking to understand one of his works? How much rather may we expect to be humbled as we meditate, and to be baffled if we think we can comprehend, the glorious

Creator himself? Is light a mystery? How much rather he who dwells in the light that no man can approach unto! We know him only as he reveals himself.

This self-revelation involves a yet greater self-concealment. There will be the manifestation of God in the voluntary condescension of his love: and there will be the necessary seclusion within the clouds of his unapproachable glory. When a finite being seeks to understand anything of the Infinite, it must always be so. There will be the fragment of truth which the student has made and is making his own, and the illimitable expanse beneath, above, and beyond him. Thus in the field of nature we read, "The works of the Lord are great, sought out of all them that have pleasure therein." Here is our knowledge. But "No ^{Psa. cxi. 2.} man," says Solomon, "can find out the work that God maketh from the beginning to the end." There is ^{Eccl. iii. 11.} the limit of our knowledge. We are invited to consider his heavens, to trace his footprints, and to regard the operations of his hands. And yet after all, "Lo! these are parts of his ways; how faint a whisper is heard of him! the thunder of his power who can understand?" So, in the majestic course of his patient ^{Job xxvi. 14.} providence we adoringly acknowledge, "Just and true are thy ways, thou King of saints:" and yet we must ^{Rev. xv. 3.} confess, "Thy way is in the sea, and thy path in the great waters, and thy footsteps are not known." ^{Psa. lxxvii. 19.}

Humble students are treading an upland path. Their horizon widens every step they take. The angels of light, standing on a higher eminence, see further than they. Still there must be a boundary line which limits angelic intuition: and whatever lies beyond that line must be a mystery to them, or, if made known to them, made known by revelation. We rebuke the want of modesty in the unlearned peasant who argues from his ignorance against the declarations of science: surely those blessed spirits would rebuke us, if we, through preconceived notions of our own, refused to credit the simple revelations of God regarding his own mysterious Being.

He reveals himself by his names, his attributes, and his acts. And, therefore, if, combined with assertions that God is one, we find three revealed in Scripture to whom the same names, attributes, and acts are ascribed, the same so far as a personal distinction allows; if we look vainly for any fourth Divine one, or any intimation of more than three; if we connect with this the intimate and necessary union affirmed to exist betwixt the Father, and the Son, and the Spirit, as when the Lord Jesus says, "I and my Father are one," and when Paul says, "The Spirit searches the depths of God;" if, then, we find that every Christian is baptized into one Name,—the Name of the Father, and of the Son, and of the Holy Ghost,—we are led swiftly and irresistibly up to the doctrine (call it by what name you will) of the Trinity in Unity.

(2) Hence, at the risk of apparent repetition, I shall bring together again some few Bible testimonies to the Deity of the Father, the Son, and the Holy Ghost; combining them in one view; and adding a further declaration from Scripture of our sole dependence on the alone Jehovah; so that you may see at a glance, that we are compelled by the Christian verity, "to acknowledge the glory of the eternal Trinity, and in the power of the Divine Majesty to worship the Unity."

Collect for
Trinity
Sunday.

I.

The Father, the Son, and the Holy Ghost are eternal.

1. I am the first, and I am the last.—Isai. xliv. 6.
The everlasting (αἰωνίου) God.—Rom. xvi. 26.

2. I am the first and the last.—Rev. i. 17. Whose
goings forth have been from of old, from everlasting (ἀπ᾽ ἀρχῆς ἐξ ἡμερῶν αἰῶνος—*LXX.*)—
Micah v. 2.

3. The eternal (αἰωνίου) Spirit.—Heb. ix. 14.

The One Eternal is our trust. The eternal God is
thy refuge, and underneath are the everlasting arms.
—Deut. xxxiii. 27.

II.

*The Father, the Son, and the Holy Ghost created all
things.*

1. One God, the Father, of whom are all things.—
1 Cor. viii. 6. The Lord.... it is he that hath
made us.—Psa. c. 3.

2. All things were made by him (the Word, etc.—
John i. 3. By him were all things created, etc.
—Col. i. 16.

3. Who hath measured, etc.—who hath directed the
Spirit of the Lord?—Isai. xl. 13. The Spirit of ^{Isaiah xl 12, 13.}
God hath made me.—Job xxxiii. 4.

The One Almighty is our trust. Commit the keeping of their souls to him,—as unto a faithful Creator.
—1 Pet. iv. 19.

III.

*The Father, the Son, and the Holy Ghost are omni-
present.*

1. Do not I fill the heaven and earth? saith the Lord.
—Jer. xxiii. 24.

2. Lo, I am with you alway.—Matt. xxviii. 20.

3. Whither shall I go from thy Spirit?—Psa.
cxxxix. 7.

The One omnipresent God is our trust. He is not
far from every one of us; for in him we live, and move,
and have our being.—Acts xvii. 27, 28.

IV.

The Father, the Son, and the Holy Ghost are incom-
prehensible and omniscient.

1. No one knoweth the Father, save the Son.—Matt.
    xi. 27.   Known unto God are all his works,
    etc.—Acts xv. 18.

2. No one knoweth the Son, save the Father.—Matt.
    xi. 27.   Lord, thou knowest all things.—John
    xxi. 17.

3. Who being his counsellor hath taught him?—
    Isai. xl. 13.   The Spirit searcheth all things.
    —1 Cor. ii. 10.

We worship the One all-seeing God. All things are
naked and opened unto the eyes of him with whom we
have to do.—Heb. iv. 13.

V.

The Father, the Son, and the Holy Ghost are true,
holy, and good.

1. He that sent me is true.—John vii. 28.   Holy
    (ἅγιε) Father.   Righteous (δίκαιε) Father.—
    John xvii. 11, 25.   The Lord is good.—Psalm
    xxxiv. 8.

2. I am . . . . the truth.—John xiv. 6.   The Holy
    One and the just (τὸν ἅγιον καὶ τὸν δίκαιον).—
    Acts iii. 14.   The good Shepherd.—John x. 11.

3. The Spirit is truth.—1 John v. 6.   The Spirit,
    the holy One.—John xiv. 26.   Thy Spirit is
    good.—Psalm cxliii. 10.

We adore the One Lord of infinite goodness. Who
shall not fear thee, O Lord, and glorify thy name?
for thou only art holy.—Rev. xv. 4.

VI.

The Father, the Son, and the Holy Ghost have each
a self-regulating will.

1. Him that worketh all things after the counsel of

his own will (τὴν βουλὴν τοῦ θελήματος).—Eph.
i. 11.

2. The Son wills (βούληται) to reveal him.—Matt.
xi. 27. Father, I will (θέλω).—John xvii. 24.

3. Dividing to every one severally as he wills (βού-
λεται)—1 Cor. xii. 11.

We rest on the will of him who alone is Jehovah.
The will of the Lord be done.—Acts xxi. 14.

VII.

The Father, the Son, and the Holy Ghost are the
fountain of life.

1. With thee is the fountain of life.—Psa. xxxvi. 9.
   God hath quickened us.—Eph. ii. 4, 5.

2. In him (the Word) was life.—John. i 4. The
   Son quickeneth whom he will.—John v. 21.

3. The Spirit is life.—Rom. viii. 10. Born of the
   Spirit.—John iii. 8.

We depend on one life-giving God. Love the Lord
thy God,...cleave unto him,...for he is thy life.
—Deut. xxx. 20.

VIII.

The Father, the Son, and the Holy Ghost strengthen,
comfort, and sanctify us.

1. Thou strengthenedst me with strength in my
   soul.—Psa. cxxxviii. 3. I will comfort you.—
   Isai. lxvi. 13.—Sanctified by God the Father.
   —Jude 1.

2. I can do all things through Christ which strength-
   eneth me.—Phil. iv. 13. If any consolation in
   Christ.—Phil. ii. 1. Sanctified in Christ Jesus.
   —1 Cor. i. 2.

3. Strengthened with might by his Spirit in the
   inner man.—Eph. iii. 16. The Comforter, the
   Holy Ghost.—John xiv. 26. Being sanctified
   by the Holy Ghost.—Rom. xv. 16.

We trust in One God for spiritual power. My God, my strength, in whom I will trust.—Psa. xviii. 2.

IX.

The Father, the Son, and the Holy Ghost fill the soul with Divine love.

1. Every one that loveth him that begat.—1 John v. 1. If any man love the world, the love of the Father is not in him.—1 John ii. 15.

2. The love of Christ constraineth us.—2 Cor. v. 14. If any man love not the Lord Jesus Christ. —1 Cor. xvi. 22.

3. I beseech you for the love of the Spirit.—Rom. xv. 30. Your love in the Spirit.—Col. i. 8.

The love of the One living and true God characterizes the saint. Thou shalt love the Lord thy God with all thy heart.—Deut. vi. 5.

X.

The Father, the Son, and the Holy Ghost gave the Divine law.

1. The law of the Lord is perfect.—Psa. xix. 7. The word of our God.—Isai. xl. 8. Thus saith the Lord God.—Ezek. ii. 4.

2. The law of Christ.—Gal. vi. 2. The word of Christ.—Col. iii. 16. These things saith the Son of God.—Rev. ii. 18.

3. The law of the Spirit of life.—Rom. viii. 2. Holy men of God spake as they were moved by the Holy Ghost.—2 Pet. i. 21. The Holy Ghost said.—Acts xiii. 2.

The word of One Legislator is the believer's rule. There is one Lawgiver who is able to save.—James iv. 12.

XI.

The Father, the Son, and the Holy Ghost dwell in the hearts of believers.

1. I will dwell in them.—2 Cor. vi. 16. God is in
   you of a truth.—1 Cor. xiv. 25. Our fellowship is with the Father.—1 John i. 3.
2. Christ may dwell in your hearts by faith.—Eph.
   iii. 17. Christ in you, the hope of glory.—Col.
   i. 27. Our fellowship......with his Son Jesus
   Christ.—1 John i. 3.
3. The Spirit dwelleth with you, and shall be in you.
   —John xiv. 17. The communion of the Holy
   Ghost.—2 Cor. xiii. 14.

The contrite heart receives One Divine guest. Thus
saith the high and lofty One that inhabiteth eternity,
I dwell with him that is of a contrite and humble
heart.—Isai. lvii. 15.

XII.

*The Father, the Son, and the Holy Ghost are, each
by himself, the supreme Jehovah and God.*

1. I am Jehovah thy God.—Ex. xx. 2. Thou,
   Lord, art most High for evermore.—Psa. xcii. 8.
2. Jehovah our God.—Isai. xl. 3, with Matt. iii. 3.
   (See pp. 72—85.) The Highest.—Luke i. 76,
   with Matt. xi. 10.
3. Jehovah God.—Ezek. viii. 1, 3. (See pp. 138—
   140). The Highest.—Luke i. 35.

*The One supreme Lord God is our God for ever and
ever.* Jehovah, our Elohim, One Jehovah.—Deut. vi. 4.

From this brief comparison, which might be elabo-
rated at far greater length, (if the reader asks for
further proof of any statement, I earnestly entreat him
to refer back to the more detailed exposition,) Scripture assures us that the Father, the Son, and the Holy
Ghost, have *the same Divine attributes,* concur with a
mind and will and heart, personally independent but
unitedly harmonious, in *the same Divine acts,* and are

Cf. Jones.

addressed by *the same Divine names*. And further, we learn that our trust is not dispersed or confused by this co-equal Godhood of the Sacred Three: but that (a way of access being opened in the gospel through the revelation of the Father in Christ by the Spirit) we rest on, we worship, and we love One God. Thus, these Three are One: or, in the language of the first Article of the Church of England—

"There is but One living and true God, everlasting; without body, parts, or passions; of infinite power, wisdom, and goodness; the Maker and Preserver of all things, both visible and invisible. And in Unity of this Godhead, there be Three persons of one substance, power and eternity; the Father, the Son, and the Holy Ghost."

(3) Are you tempted to say, "such a brief article as this enunciated by Christ himself, and recorded by the apostles, would have settled every controversy for ever: why, oh why, was it not contained in Scripture?" Haply, Elihu might quell the rising suspicion, "Behold, in this thou art not just: I will answer thee, that God is greater than man. Why dost thou strive against him? for he giveth not account of any of his matters. For God speaketh once, yea twice, but man

Job xxxiii.
12–14.

perceiveth it not." But it is by no means certain that such an article would have settled every doubt. It would have been handed down from age to age: many manuscripts must needs be collated: possibly some obscure variation might be discovered. But even if the text were as impregnable as the opening of John's Gospel, I doubt whether it would have convinced such minds as remain unconvinced of the Deity of Christ, after weighing those transparent de-

Eph. ii. 8.

clarations. Saving faith is the gift of God. Granting, however, that it had materially shortened the path by which sincere inquirers attain the true faith, (for Scripture assures us that none, who heartily seek the Lord, stop short of Jesus Christ,) what would have been its effect on the church at large?   Permit me here to quote some admirable remarks from "Cautions for the Times."

There is another reason against the providing in Scripture of a regular systematic statement of Christian doctrines. Supposing such a summary of gospel truths had been drawn up, and could have been contrived with such exquisite skill as to be sufficient and well adapted for all, of every age and country, what would have been the probable result? It would have commanded the unhesitating assent of all Christians, who would, with deep veneration, have stored up the very words of it in their memory, without any need of laboriously searching the rest of the Scriptures, to ascertain its agreement with them; which is what we do (at least, are evidently called on to do) with a human exposition of the faith; and the absence of this labour, together with the tranquil security as to the correctness of their belief, which would have been thus generated, would have ended in a careless and contented apathy.   There would have been.... no call for vigilant attention in the investigation of truth—none of that effort of mind which is now requisite, in comparing one passage with another, and collecting instruction from the scattered, oblique, and incidental references to various doctrines in the existing Scriptures; and in consequence none of that excitement of the best feelings, and that improvement of the heart, which are the natural and, doubtless, the designed result of an humble, diligent, and sincere study of the Christian Scriptures.

In fact all study, properly so called, of the rest of Scripture—all lively interest in its perusal—would have nearly been superseded by such an inspired compendium of doctrine; to which alone, as by far the most convenient for that purpose, habitual reference would have been made in any question that might arise.   Both would have been regarded indeed as of Divine authority; but the compendium as the fused and purified metal;

the other as the mine containing the crude ore. And the compendium itself being not, like the existing Scriptures, that *from which* the faith is to be learned, but *the very thing to be learned,* would have come to be regarded by most with an indolent, unthinking veneration, which would have exercised little or no influence on the character. Their orthodoxy would have been as it were petrified; like the bodies of those animals we read of incrusted in the ice of the polar regions—firm fixed, indeed, and preserved unchangeable; but cold, motionless, lifeless. It is only when our energies are roused, and faculties exercised, and our attention kept awake by an ardent pursuit of truth, and anxious watchfulness against error—when, in short, we feel ourselves to be doing something towards acquiring, or retaining, or improving our knowledge—it is then only that that knowledge makes the requisite practical impression on the heart and on the conduct.

To the church, then, has her all-wise Founder left the office of *teaching*—to the Scriptures, that of proving the Christian doctrine: to the Scriptures, he has left the delineation of Christian *principles*—to each church, the *application* of those principles, in their symbols or articles of religion—in their forms of worship —and in their ecclesiastical regulations,—pp. **443, 444.**

How beautiful is the analogy here between the word of God and the natural creation! Had we been told that the earth was to be so arranged that eight hundred millions of human beings could live thereon, should we not, in thought, have done away with the vast unproductive forests, the superfluous mountains, the exorbitant ocean, and have divided it into so many plots for agriculture, like the veriest pauper field? This was not God's way. The woods, and hills, and seas minister to the clouds, and the clouds drop fatness on the fertile fields and the luxurious plain; and thus he opens his hand and supplies all things living with plenteousness. So is it with the

Scriptures of truth. We should, perhaps, have expected definitions, and articles, and formularies, and
canons, and creeds. This was not God's method.

There is the incident of touching simplicity, the
solemn majesty of law, the flame of patriotic zeal, the
heart-experience which speaks to our heart, the grand-
est poetry, the most magnificent songs of praise, the
rapid changes on the prophetic harp, the inimitable
story of redeeming love, the calm deductions of logical
argument, the echo of angelic joy, the unbarring of
the gates of glory, and the reflection of the light of
eternity. And yet, amid all these manifold combina-
tions, the simple rule of our faith in the One living
and true God—Father, Son, and Spirit, the source of
creation, redemption and sanctification,—is marked
out with a precision that "he may run that readeth." ^{Heb. ii; 2.}

But, do you ask, is it needful for every believer to
pass through such a long process of proof as even this
little treatise sets forth? Assuredly not. The Bible
is eminently the poor man's book. These things are
hidden from the wise and prudent, and revealed unto
babes. And to such a childlike mind a very few ^{Matt. xi. 25; xviii. 3.}
simple truths generally carry conviction, and with
conviction life and peace. "I am God, and beside me
there is no Saviour." "Behold the Lamb of God, which
taketh away the sin of the world." "I will send the
Comforter to you." His Father, his Redeemer, his
Sanctifier, are equally indispensable to him: and he
knows that he was baptized into the name of the
Father, the Son, and the Holy Ghost. He needs no
more. Without any laboured syllogisms, he believes
these Three are One. The truths finds him. He does
not expect to fathom the mystery; but his whole heart
embraces that which satisfied his whole necessity.

If, however, doubts and suspicions assail these first

1 Pet. iii. 15.

Jer. xxix. 11-13.

principles when implanted, or keep back an inquirer from believing them, then the word of God, reverently consulted, affords a complete answer to every, what I may call, rational objection. The armoury supplies a weapon for every encounter. We are ready to give every man a reason of the hope that is in us. Therefore, if held back by these doubts from faith in Christ, you must give yourself, heart and soul, to this momentous inquiry; you must shake off that deadly indifference which would leave this question undecided; you must watch and pray; and then be assured the promise shall never fail.—"I know the thoughts that I think toward you, saith the Lord, thoughts of peace and not of evil, to give you an expected end. Then shall ye call upon me, and ye shall go and pray unto me, and I will hearken unto you; and ye shall seek me, and find me, when ye shall search for me with all your heart."

Mortal life, stretching forth into immortality, is to each man like a precious cabinet stored with priceless jewels. But the cabinet is locked, and to those without Christ the key is wanting. The gospel is that key. It is proffered to all. How many, alas, carelessly thrust it aside! But some, you may think with a modest caution, refuse to make the trial, lest haply they should hamper the lock, until they have been assured by a careful sifting of documents, by a comparing of outlines of the hidden wards with the key, and by other infallible proofs, that the key in question was the one made and designed for the cabinet. This investigation they pursue with untiring assiduity, until, satisfied of the credibility of the evidence adduced, they try the bolt with a trembling hand; it yields to the touch and the cabinet is their own: they are rich for ever. Many others, however, have more trustful-ness, and less fearfulness. They feel their poverty; they believe the offer is to be relied on; they know that many of their neighbours have found it so; and without further delay they also try the lock: it yields, and the cabinet is theirs. You can never argue them out of their persuasion that the key they hold in their hands is the key of the cabinet. No other unlocks it; and this does. That is enough for them. They may not have so intelligent a knowledge of the way in which that elaborate key turns back one secret spring after another: that knowledge, whenever acquired, belongs to the patient, pains-taking investigator: but both alike possess the jewels.

So is it with the gospel of Jesus Christ: it exactly fits the intricate wards of the human heart. It unlocks the inestimable treasures of human life. He that uses it is rich indeed; rich towards God; rich for eternity. Whether he has been led to faith in Christ through long and painful inquiries, as may be the case especially with those who have much time for thought, and keen intellectual powers; or whether with a more confiding alacrity, which is the experience of most Christians, (for "God hath chosen the poor of this world rich in faith,") he has obeyed the gospel at once, the life-giving efficacy is the same. "As many as received him, to them gave he power to become the sons of God." The question is one of obedience or of disobedience. "The mystery [of the gospel of Jesus Christ] is now according to the commandment of the everlasting God made known to all nations, for THE OBEDIENCE OF FAITH." Obedience is life; "He that believeth on the Son hath everlasting life:" and disobedience is death; for the same Scripture continues, "He that believeth not the Son shall not see life; but the wrath of God abideth on him."

James ii. 5.

John i. 12.

Rom. xvi. 25, 26.

John iii. 36.

(4) Do you say, Is not a trustful knowledge of God the Father sufficient? Scripture answers, There is no true knowledge of God the Father, except in God the Son: for Jesus Christ says, "I am the way, the truth, and the life; no man cometh unto the Father, but by me."   And John writes, "Whosoever denieth the Son, the same hath nòt the Father."   And again, "Whosoever transgresseth, and abideth not in the doctrine of Christ, hath not God. He that abideth in the doctrine of Christ, he hath both the Father and the Son."   Now Scripture has proved to us the co-essential Godhood of the Son with the Father: and, if once the Holy Spirit convince you of this, you will be the first to ask, what can denial of the Son be, if to deny his Deity be not this negation?   With your keen sense of honour, you will then be the first to acknowledge that such denial destroys the glory of his person; tears the crown from his brow; empties the atonement of its virtue; and, however undesignedly, charges the church of Christ with idolatry, and the word of God with equivocation and untruthfulness. For he who denies the Deity of our Lord "believeth not the record that God hath given of his Son." There are indeed many, who, professedly believing the Deity of the Son of God, by their works deny him: theirs, perhaps, is an aggravated guilt:—but those who professedly disbelieve his Deity, seeing that such unbelief extracts all saving efficacy from his work, are rejecting the only "name under heaven given among men, whereby we must be saved."

Further, do you say, God is love, and will not visit with eternal condemnation the creatures of his hand? My friends, you are making to yourselves a God of your own imagination, a God of mercy and compassion only, but without holy jealousy and righteousness.

John xiv. 6.
1 John ii. 23.
2 John 9.
1 John v. 10.
Acts iv. 12.

Such a one is not the God of creation, or of providence, or of the Bible. He is not the God of creation;
for even there, amid the abounding evidence of his
goodness, there are things which tell of his severity;
there is not only the sunshine, and the summer, and
the dew, and the calm,—but also the terrible darkness,
and the wintry blast, and the storm, and the volcano.
Such a one is not the God of permissive providence;
for there is not only the happy home, and prattling
childhood, and the mart of peaceful merchandise, and
the honourable senate,—but also the chamber of suffering, and the creeping infirmities of age, and the
wail of oppression, and the battle-field strewn with
corpses. Nor is such a one the God of the Bible:
God is love indeed—but love embraces all his attributes, not mercy only, but righteousness likewise:
"for love is strong as death, jealousy is hard as the
grave, the coals thereof are coals of fire, which hath a
most vehement flame." Oh, surely not in vain was Song viii. 6. See margin.
the cry of the gospel herald, "Flee from the wrath to
come." Not in vain the warning of Jesus Christ, "If Matt. iii. 7.
ye believe not that I am *he*, ye shall die in your sins." John viii. 24.
Not in vain the awakening question of Peter, "What
shall the end be of them that obey not the gospel of
God?" 1 Pet. iv. 17.

It is so often asserted that the inflexible righteousness manifested under the old dispensation, as in the
deluge, in the destruction of the cities of the plain, in
the plagues on Egypt, or in the chastisements on
Israel, has been modified by the "milder genius of the
gospel"—though they who make the assertion forget, See Luke xvii. 36—38.
that these cases are adduced as examples in the New Rom. ix. 17.
Testament,—that I bring before you in the note below* 1 Cor. x. 6-11.

---

* *Testimony under the new covenant to the righteous severity of God.*
Matt. iii. 7-12, John Baptist warns to flee from the wrath to come.

some portion of the witness of the New Testament to the immutable justice of God. I fully grant you that

---

Matt. v. 26—29, Jesus speaks of the eternal prison, and of the unholy being cast into hell.

— vii. 13, of the broad way leading to destruction; and ver. 23, of the hour when he will say, Depart from me.

.[These last are taken from the sermon on the mount, in which the Fatherly character of God shines as a golden thread interwoven throughout.]

— viii. 12, the children of the kingdom cast out into outer darkness.

— x. 15, more tolerable for Sodom in the day of judgment; and ver. 28, "Fear him which is able to destroy both soul and body in hell."

[This last in closest connection with filial trust towards God.]

— xi. 20—24, the woes on Chorazin.

— xii. 32, the unpardonable sin.

— xiii. 41, 42, 49, 50, the judgment of the wicked.

— xviii. 6—9, the end of those who cause offences.

— xxi. 44, the stone falling on the disobedient.

— xxii. 13, the guest expelled into outer darkness.

— xxiii. the woes on the Pharisees.

— xxiv. the foretold destruction of Jerusalem, typical of the last judgment

— xxv. 12, the foolish virgins disowned; ver. 30 the unprofitable servant cast out; ver. 41, the sentence upon those on the left hand—"Depart from me, ye cursed, into everlasting fire, prepared for the devil and his angels."

Mark xvi. 16, after the resurrection, the same inflexible law— "He that believeth and is baptized shall be saved; but he that believeth not shall be damned."

Luke xii. 46, the unfaithful servant's end.

— xiii. 28, a scene of future remorse sketched, which the prescient Christ alone could sketch.

— xvi. 22, 23, "the rich man also died and was buried; and in hell he lifted up his eyes, being in torments."

— xvii. 26—30, the deluge and the destruction of Sodom, types of the end of the wicked at the second Advent.

John iii. 18, the unbeliever condemned already; and ver. 36, "the wrath of God abideth on him."

now God is withholding his judgments: it is the day
of grace, it is the time of love, the goodness of God

John v. 29, the resurrection of damnation.
— viii. 24, ye shall die in your sins.
Acts iii. 23, the disobedient soul destroyed.
— v. 1—11, the judgment on Ananias and Sapphira.
— xiii. 40, 41, see the peroration of Paul's sermon at Antioch:
— xxviii. 25—27, and of his address to the Jews.
Rom. i. 18, the wrath of God revealed against all ungodliness.
— ii. 4—11, wrath treasured up against the day of wrath;—
      indignation and wrath, tribulation and anguish, ren-
      dered to every evil doer.
— vi. 23, the wages of sin is death.
— xii. 19, "Vengeance is mine; I will repay, saith the Lord."
1 Cor. iii. 17, if any man, etc., him shall God destroy.
— vi. 9, "the unrighteous shall not inherit the kingdom of
      God."
— xvi. 22, "If any man love not the Lord Jesus Christ, let
      him be Anathema Maranatha."
2 Cor. ii. 16, to them that perish we are the savour of death unto
      death.
— iv. 3, the gospel hid in them that are lost.
Gal. i. 8, the solemn anathema on those who pervert the gospel.
— vi. 8, he that soweth to his flesh......reaping corruption.
Eph. ii. 3, we were children of wrath.
Phil. iii. 18, 19, "I tell you, even weeping, that they are the ene-
      mies of the cross of Christ: whose end is destruction."
2 Thess. i. 7—9, the Lord Jesus shall be revealed from heaven
      "in flaming fire, taking vengeance on them that know
      not God, and that obey not the gospel of our Lord Jesus
      Christ; who shall be punished with an everlasting de-
      struction. . . ."
— ii. 12, "that they all might be damned who believed not
      the truth."
Heb. ii. 3, "How shall we escape, if we neglect so great salvation?"
— x. 27—31, "a certain fearful looking for of judgment and fiery
      indignation, which shall devour the adversaries........
      It is a fearful thing to fall into the hands of the living God."
— xii. 29, "for our God is a consuming fire."
James ii. 10, "Whosoever shall keep the whole law, and yet
      offend in one point, he is guilty of all."

Luke xiii. 25.

Prov. i. 28.

Heb. xii. 21.

leadeth us to repentance: but the season is limited, and "when once the master of the house is risen up, and hath shut to the door," then the last hour of pardoning mercy will have passed away, and he whose name is love declares, "Then shall they call upon me, but I will not answer; they shall seek me early, but they shall not find me." But if Jesus wept, when foretelling the judgments on Jerusalem, well may the heart of a poor pardoned sinner bleed, to gather such cumulative proof of his holy indignation. So terrible is the evidence that, like Moses at Sinai, "I exceedingly fear and quake." If it were only one isolated passage, you might urge it was figurative language; but here

---

1 Pet. ii. 8, [Jesus Christ] "a stone of stumbling, and a rock of offence, even to them which stumble at the word, being disobedient: whereunto also they were appointed."

1 Pet. iv. 17, 18, "what shall the end be of them that obey not the gospel of God?......where shall the ungodly and the sinner appear?"

2 Pet. ii. 17, "to whom the mist of darkness is reserved for ever."

— iii. 7, the day of judgment and perdition of ungodly men.

1 John v. 19, the whole world lieth in wickedness.

Jude 14, 15, the Lord cometh....to execute judgment.

Rev. vi. 16, hide us from the face of him that sitteth on the throne, and from the wrath of the Lamb.

— xix. 3, her smoke rose up for ever and ever.

— " 15, "and out of his mouth goeth forth a sharp sword, that with it he should smite the nations; and he shall rule them with a rod of iron, and he treadeth the wine-press of the fierceness and wrath of Almighty God."

— xx. 15, "and whosoever was not found written in the book of life was cast into the lake of fire."

— xxi. 8, "but the fearful, and unbelieving, and the abominable, and murderers, and whoremongers, and idolaters, and all liars, shall have their part in the lake which burneth with fire and brimstone: which is the second death...."

— xxii. 11, "he that is unjust, let him be unjust still; and he that is filthy, let him be filthy still."

it is written in history, prophecy, sermon, epistle, vision,—all alike proving that our God is a consuming fire, and that of the enemies of the cross the end is destruction. I repeat, you may conceive a God of compassion only, and fall down and worship him, but such a one is not the righteous Judge of all the earth: and you may beautify the name of the Father, whom you adore, with every trait of benevolence, and tenderness, and grace; but it is not the name of the one living and true God, for that is the name of the Father, and of the Son, and of the Holy Ghost.

God forbid that I should write with anything of bitterness or pride. I feel far too deeply for that. You will not accuse me of it. Shipwrecked in one common fall with us, you have adopted principles of your own, and staked your immortality of weal or woe upon them. We have embarked upon that we *know* to be the only true life-boat: and with all the importunity of affection, those kindlings of common humanity which bind us together, we cry to you— "Friends, that raft of your own construction cannot survive the tempest. Come with us. Yet there is room. Yet there is time. Our life-boat cannot sink. Our pilot knows the port."

Let us recur to our position before God, as sketched from Scripture in the opening of this treatise. The Bible represented us as guilty, strengthless, and in darkness. Whatever moral excellences may adorn us in the sight of man; philanthropy, generosity, tenderness, integrity—still the penetrating law, the law of perfect love, reveals innumerable violations of our nearest and noblest duties. We are sinners; and as sinners, exposed to all this righteous wrath in the day of wrath.

Once realize this, and our false peace is broken up

for ever. Our earthly gayety is gone. Life, without our Father's smile, is nor worth the living. It is to flit through a mazy labyrinth of pain and pleasure, to foster affections which must wither to their roots, and to cherish hopes which must expire one by one. The irrepressible question rises again to our lips, What must I do to be saved? Where shall we find a hiding-place? "The name of the Lord is a strong tower: the righteous runneth into it, and is safe." What is his name?—the same that Moses heard in the cleft of the rock—"The LORD, the LORD God, merciful and gracious, long-suffering, and abundant in goodness and truth, keeping mercy for thousands, forgiving iniquity and transgression and sin, and that will by no means clear the guilty; visiting the iniquity of the fathers upon the children, and upon the children's children, unto the third and to the fourth generation."

How then can he clear us, the guilty? For "we are all as an unclean thing, and all our righteousnesses are as filthy rags; and we all do fade as a leaf; and our iniquities, like the wind, have taken us away." May the Lord of his sovereign mercy impress his own reply on my heart and on yours, by the power of the Holy Ghost.

Prov. xviii. 10.

Exod. xxxiv. 6, 7.

Isai. lxiv. 6.

Now we know that what things soever the law saith, it saith to them who are under the law; that every mouth may be stopped, and all the world may become guilty before God. Therefore by the deeds of the law there shall no flesh be justified in his sight; for by the law is the knowledge of sin.

But now the righteousness of God without the law is manifested, being witnessed by the law and the prophets; even the righteousness of God, which is by faith of Jesus Christ unto all and upon all them that believe: for there is no difference;

For all have sinned, and come short of the glory of God;

being justified freely by his grace, through the redemption that
is in Christ Jesus:

Whom God hath set forth to be a propitiation through faith
in his blood, to declare his righteousness for the remission of sins
that are past, through the forbearance of God; to declare, I say,
at this time, his righteousness: that he might be just, and the
justifier of him which believeth in Jesus.—*Rom.* iii. 19—26.

How blessed, how Divine a salvation! Another has
offered an atoning sacrifice for our sins; another imparts his righteousness to all who believe. The claims
of the law are satisfied; for a Victim of infinite worth
has satisfied them. Emmanuel, God with us, is surety Rom. v. 6.
for us. Christ died for the ungodly, the Just for the 1 Pet. iii. 18.
unjust, that he might bring us to God. "It is the blood
which maketh an atonement for the soul:" not the Lev. xvii. 11.
blood of bulls and of goats, but the blood of Jesus Heb. x. 4.
Christ his Son cleanseth us from all sin. And now 1 John i. 7.
God in Christ reconciles the world unto himself, not
imputing their trespasses unto them. And we are
ambassadors for Christ; as though God did beseech you
by us, we pray you in Christ's stead be ye reconciled
to God; for he hath made him who knew no sin to be
sin for us, that we might be made the righteousness of
God in him. O unexampled love! The Father sent 2 Cor. v. 19-
21.
the Son to be the Saviour of the world. God the Fa- 1 John iv. 14.
ther loving us with everlasting love: God the Son
incarnate, crucified, risen, glorified, interceding. Here
"Mercy and truth are met together; righteousness
and peace have kissed each other." Psa. lxxxv. 10.

But once more: "Jesus says, No one can come unto
me except the Father which hath sent me draw him. John vi. 44.
And yet again: "No one cometh unto the Father, but
by me." It is a circle of light and love. We go John xiv. 6.
round about it. How are we to enter it? Jesus
answers, "When the Comforter is come, whom I will

John xv. 26.
send unto you from the Father, he shall testify of me.
xvi. 13, 14.
. . . he will guide you into all truth. . . . he shall receive of mine, and shall show it unto you." Here is
the power of entrance. That which is born of the
Spirit is spirit.

Oh, blessed new-born soul! washed in the blood of
Christ, clothed in his spotless goodness, drawn by his
quickening Spirit, it is brought to the footstool of the
throne of paternal love. It lives. It loves. All the
affections gush forth from a well of water springing
up into everlasting life. The Trinity in Unity is no
longer an abstract doctrine alone, but it interpene-
trates our spiritual being. The Father and the Son
have come unto us, and in the communion of the
See John xiv.
23.
Spirit make their abode with us: and thus dwelling in
love we dwell in God, for God is LOVE.

(5) God is love. Many, from these words alone,
have argued the necessity of a co-eternal and a co-
equal plurality in unity, as a deduction from that
absolute perfection of the Divine nature which requires every possible excellence: *co-eternal;*—for love
implies, at least, that there be One who loves, and One
who being loved reciprocates that love; and, therefore,
if the Son were not from everlasting (as the Father
himself), the first and the last, the beginning and the
ending; then before the creation of our world, or of
any worlds, through the receding cycles of a past
eternity, they have contended that "the Divine mind
would have stood in an immense solitariness," without
reciprocity of affection, and without communion of
intellectual enjoyment; and *co-equal;*—for love in its
perfection requires similarity and indeed equality of
nature, (as God records of Adam in Paradise, "there
Gen. ii. 20.
was not found a help meet for him,") and, therefore,

whatever you take away from either the one who
loves or the one who is loved, however you disparage
either in comparison of the other, you so far destroy
the propriety and completeness of the definition "*God
is Love.*"*

---

* See Alford's sermons on Divine Love: and P. Smith's Testimony, Appendix III., from which some of the clauses in the
above paragraph are taken.

The following beautiful extracts from a German treatise, by
Sartorius, have been translated and sent me by a friend.

"That which is asserted in theological compendiums with abstract and often negative precision of the Being and attributes of
God, is gathered together in a living, comprehensive, and fertile
idea, in that great dictum of the apostle, GOD IS LOVE. This saying of the Holy Spirit comes from the depths of the Godhead. It
is the Divine axiom beyond which we cannot fathom, and from
which all flows; the first principle of our science, as well as the
basis of our life. The first article of our creed expresses this: God
the Father is equal to 'God is love.'

[He then contrasts the two opposites *I* and *thou*, with the false
opposites of some modern philosophy, *I* and *not I.*]

"Love presupposes consciousness—personality: in the true
sense we cannot love a thing; only persons can love or truly be
loved. In the Higher Divine sense, love is the unity or union of
two distinct personalities. And this in the Highest sense the
Triune God is, the Father, the Son, and the Holy Spirit of Love.
...... 'God is love:'—whatever we may say of God's spiritual,
infinite, eternal Being; of his all-might and all-wisdom; of his
holiness, justice, and truth; of his glory and blessedness; it it
not all gathered up in the idea of absolute love? How little is
said in asserting that God is a Spirit, if his mere negative imma-
teriality and invisibility are meant: or when thinking and willing
are ascribed to him, without any character to determine the
quality of this thinking and willing. Love is spirit, is light, and
life; is conscious, personal life, not merely subjectively absorbed
in itself, but expanding, and manifesting, and objectively com-
municating itself; filling all with itself, and gathering all unto itself. Infinite and eternal are mere negative abstractions, if they

But leaving this most profound mystery, and taking with you those living truths which are necessary to our salvation, I pray you now to return to the study of the sacred volume. You will look in vain for any formal creed: but what is infinitely more valuable to the earnest student and the docile believer, you will find the threefold and yet united work of the ever blessed God,—Father, Son, and Spirit,—on our behalf.

If we ask, Whence came I, and to whom do I belong? the Bible answers we are the creatures of God the Father, of whom are all things; of God the Son, by whom all things were made; of God the Spirit, who gave us life: of these Three who are One in essence, and who in unity of counsel determined, "Let us make man in our image."

Gen. i. 26.

If, feeling our low and lost estate, we cry, What must I do to be saved? Jesus answers, "Ye must be born again. That which is born of the Spirit is spirit. —For God so loved the world that he gave his only-

---

are not contemplated as filled with love, whose nature it is to have no limits, and 'never to fail.'

"Holiness, what is it but Holy love, which only wills the holy and the good (the God-like), and abhors the evil (ungodly) because it brings ruin? And righteousness, what is it but the order, the law of love and its execution? God is love, not only as Creator and Preserver of the world, but in himself, from eternity, eternal love in person, and surely in more than One person; for love consists in the unity of [at least] two persons. The subject of love is not conceivable without the object, nor personal love without a personal object; without which it would be but self-seeking. The *I* must have a *Thou:* the eternal *I* an eternal *Thou:* eternal love an eternal object."

I give the above fragments for their intrinsic worth, without pledging myself to all the sentiments of an essay which I have not read.

begotten Son, that whosoever believeth in him should not perish, but have eternal life." John iii. 6-16.

If now craving that new birth we begin to long for that Spirit with indescribable desire, our Lord assures us, "I will pray the Father; and he shall give you another Comforter, that he may abide with you for ever." John xiv. 16.

If we ask how this, so great a salvation, was accomplished, the apostle replies, "Christ, through the Eternal Spirit, offered himself, without spot, to God;" and thus "his blood purges our conscience from dead works to serve the living and true God." Heb. ix. 14.

If we draw nigh to that great High Priest, crying, Lord, save me or I perish; He answers, "The Spirit of the Lord God is upon me; because the Lord hath anointed me to preach good tidings unto the meek; he hath sent me to bind up the broken-hearted, to proclaim liberty to the captives, and the opening of the prison to them that are bound; to proclaim the acceptable year of the Lord." Isai. lxi. 1, 2.

If we turn to the pages of the gospel histories, and humbly ask for some manifestation of this stupendous mystery, we read—"Jesus being baptized, and praying, the heaven was opened, and the Holy Ghost descended in a bodily shape like a dove upon him, and a voice came from heaven, which said, Thou art my beloved Son: in thee I am well pleased." Luke iii. 21, 22.

If, as we ponder the threefold benediction pronounced on the worshipping Israelites,—"The Lord bless thee and keep thee: the Lord make his face shine upon thee, and be gracious unto thee: the Lord lift up his countenance upon thee, and give thee peace:"—and observe how this threefold blessing mysteriously coalesced in one covenant name, for it is added, "They shall put my name upon the children of Israel, and I will bless them:" if, pondering these things, we cry, Bless Num. vi. 23-27.

me, even me also, O my Father; we shall hear a still small voice saying to us, The blessings of that name into which you were baptized be yours in deed and in truth, and in the power of spiritual life, "the name of the Father, and of the Son, and of the Holy Ghost."

If emboldened, we would now interpret this more plainly, the doctrine drops as the rain, and distils as the dew, in the benediction of the new covenant. "The grace of the Lord Jesus Christ, and the love of God, and the communion of the Holy Spirit, be with you. Amen."

2 Cor. xiii. 14.

We betake ourselves to prayer; how easy the new and living way! "Through Jesus we have access by one Spirit unto the Father." And while kneeling at the throne of grace how deep the fellowship: "The Spirit itself beareth witness with our spirit, that we are the children of God: and if children, then heirs; heirs of God, and joint-heirs with Christ."

Eph. ii. 18.

Rom. viii. 16, 17.

If we are ever tempted to draw back from the hope of the gospel, how awful does the provocation of the Triune Jehovah appear when Scripture, warning us of the wrath to come, demands—"Of how much sorer punishment, suppose ye, shall he be thought worthy, who hath trodden under foot the Son of God, and hath counted the blood of the covenant, wherewith he was sanctified, an unholy thing, and hath done despite unto the Spirit of grace? For we know him that hath said, Vengeance belongeth unto me, I will recompense, saith the Lord."

Heb. x. 29, 30.

We are stablished in the faith: but we long to see this great mystery in living connection with the communion of saints, with the better covenant of promise, and with all the framework of human society:—this too is vouchsafed: for we read, "There is one body, and one Spirit. even as ye are called in one hope of your calling; one Lord, one faith, one baptism, one God and Father of all, who is above all, and through all, and in you all." *Eph. iv. 4–6.*

Now we see that all things are ours, who are "elect according to the foreknowledge of God the Father, through sanctification of the Spirit, unto obedience and sprinkling of the blood of Jesus Christ;" for *1 Pet. i. 2.* what, in the confidence of faith we ask, shall separate us from the love of God, who "hath from the beginning chosen us to salvation through sanctification of the Spirit and belief of the truth,......to the obtaining of the glory of our Lord Jesus Christ?" *2 Thess. ii. 13, 14.*

This assurance of faith is no idle self-confidence, for we hear the apostle's earnest entreaty: "But ye, beloved, building up yourselves on your most holy faith, praying in the Holy Ghost, keep yourselves in the love of God, looking for the mercy of our Lord Jesus Christ unto eternal life." *Jude 20, 21.*

And is now the need of our soul irrepressible for suitable language in which to express the adoring gratitude of our hearts, let us fall low on our faces with the veiled seraphim, and cry, "Holy, holy, holy, is the Lord of hosts. Holy, holy, holy, Lord God *Isai. vi. 2, 3.* Almighty, which was, and is, and is to come." *Rev. iv. 8.*

Yes, the pure white light which fills the firmament of heaven, and imbues the clouds with brightness, and paints the inimitable beauty of every colour which delights us, is only a faint emblem of that glorious name —the name of the Father, and of the Son, and of the Holy Ghost—which alone can penetrate the depths of the human heart; which alone irradiates the mysteries of time and the darkness of the shadow of death; and *Ezek. i. 28.* which has spanned the throne of the Eternal with the emerald rainbow of everlasting peace. *Rev. iv. 3.*

And here I must close. At the beginning of this

essay I ventured to allude to past personal conflicts. My faith was sorely tried; and I often thought, as many others have done, that Satan exhausted his quiver on my battered shield. But unutterably painful as those days of struggle were to me, I should number them among the most golden of my life, if they taught me to remove one obstacle from the path of those who are feeling after Jesus, my Saviour and my God. I was at times constrained to cry in bitterness of soul, "All thy billows are gone over me," though an unseen hand kept me clinging to Him who was my life, like the limpet to the rock, buffeted by every wave of the fretting sea. But gladly shall I have suffered the tempest, if God may enable me thereby to stretch forth a helping hand to those who are sinking in the deep waters, until their feet are planted on the Rock of Ages. Then shall we shortly stand together in his presence, where is fulness of joy, and cast our crowns before him on whose head are many crowns, and sing the everlasting song, "Unto him that loved us, and washed us from our sins in his own blood, and hath made us kings and priests unto God and his Father, to him be glory and dominion for ever and ever." The Lord, of his infinite mercy, grant this by the power of the Holy Ghost, for Jesus Christ's sake. Amen and Amen.

SCRIPTURE INDEX

To have tabulated all the verses quoted in the Essay would have made this Index far too voluminous. I have therefore only noted those passages more particularly discussed or illustrated. These however will, I hope, with the full summary of the argument given in the table of Contents, afford a sufficient clue to the rest.

		PAGE
Genesis i. 1	Elohim created	(note) 145
— — 26	Let us make	145, 172
— iii. 15	The seed of the woman	31, 97
— vi. 3	My Spirit	138
— xxxii. 30	I have seen God face to face	53
Exodus xxxiii. 20	Thou canst not see my face	53
— xxxiv. 6, 7	The name of the Lord	168
— — 14	Whose name is Jealous	20
Leviticus xvii. 11	It is the blood	169
Numbers vi. 23—27	The Lord bless thee	173
— xi. 17	Take of the Spirit	123
Deut. vi. 4, 5	Jehovah our Elohim	76, (note) 146, 154, 155
— xxx. 20	He is thy life	153
— xxxiii. 27	The Eternal God thy refuge	151
Judges vi. 24	Jehovah Shalom	55
2 Samuel xxiii. 2	The Spirit of the Lord	139
Nehemiah ix. 5—7		23, 41
— — 27	Saviours who saved them	110, 115
Job xxxiii. 12—14	He giveth not account	156
Psalm ii. 2—12		32, 97
— xviii. 2	My God my strength	154
— xlix. 7, 8, 15	None can redeem, etc.	20
— xc. 1—6	Thou hast been our dwelling	19
— xcv. 6—9	Let us worship, etc.	133
— cx. 1—7		97
— cxxxvi. 1—4	Jehovah alone doeth great wonders	139
— cxxxix. 7	Go from thy Spirit	128
Isaiah i. 2	I have nourished	14

23

			PAGE
Isaiah vi. 5 ..	Mine eyes have seen ..	..	.. 53, 73
— — 8 ..	.. ..	..	(note) 145
— vii. 14 ..	.. ..	..	.. 32
— viii. 13, 14	A stone of stumbling ..	..	.. 73
— ix. 6 ..	.. ..	..	.. 32, 98
— xi. 2—4 ..	The Spirit of Jehovah	..	98 (note) 121
— xxv. 8 ..	He will swallow up death	..	.. 45
— xxxi. 1—6	Men and not God ..	..	.. 19
— xxxii. 2 ..	A man shall be a covert	..	.. 48
— xl. 3 ..	Prepare ye the way of Jehovah ..	..	.. 72
— — 12, 14 ..	Who hath directed the Spirit	..	.. 130, 151
— xlii. 8 ..	My glory will I not ..	..	.. 22
— xlv. 15 ..	A God that hidest thyself	..	.. 12
— — 19 ..	I said not, Seek me in vain	..	.. 12
— — 21—25	.. ..	..	16, 46, 74
— xlviii. 16 ..	The Lord God and his Spirit sent me	..	91
— li. 12—15	I, even I, etc. ..	..	.. 19
— liii. 1—12	.. ..	..	32, 33, 98, 103
— liv. 5 ..	Thy Maker is thy husband	..	49 (note) 145
— lvii. 15 ..	The high and lofty One	..	.. 155
— lxi. 1 ..	The Spirit of the Lord on me	..	(note) 122, 173
— lxiii. 10—14	They vexed his Holy Spirit	..	.. 138
Jeremiah xvii. 5—8	Cursed be the man, etc.	..	.. 22, 86
— xxiii. 6 ..	The Lord our righteousness	..	.. 32, 46
Ezekiel i. 26—28	.. ..	..	32, 55, 176
— xx. 11, 12	My statutes ..	..	.. 14
— xxxvii. 9—14	Come, O breath ..	..	.. 133
Daniel ix. 24—26	Messiah. ..	..	.. 32
Hosea xii. 3, 4 ..	Power with God ..	..	.. 53, 54
Micah v. 2 ..	From everlasting ..	..	26, 40, 151
Haggai ii 7 ..	The desire of all nations	..	.. 32
Zech. iii. 9, and iv. 10	Seven eyes ..	..	(note) 121
— xii. 10 ..	He whom they pierced	..	.. 73
— xiii. 7 ..	My fellow ..	..	.. 98
— xiv. 9 ..	One Lord ..	..	.. 76
Malachi iv. 2 ..	The Sun of righteousness	..	.. 32
Matthew iii. 3 ..	Prepare ye the way ..	..	.. 72
— iv. 6 ..	It is written ..	..	.. 10
— — 10 ..	Thou shalt worship ..	..	.. 66
— v. 26, 29	.. ..	..	(note) 164
— — 48 ..	Be perfect even as :.	..	.. 112
— vi. 9—13	The Lord's prayer ..	..	.. 46, 47
— vii. 13, 23	.. ..	..	.. 164

			PAGE
Matthew viii. 2 ..	Lord, if thou wilt		58
— — 25 ..	Lord, save us		58
— ix. 18 ..	Come and lay thy hand		58
— xi. 27 ..	He to whom the Son ..		28, 109, 113
— xii. 32 ..	Speaketh against the Holy Ghost		126
— xiv. 33 ..	Of a truth thou art		58
— xv. 25 ..	Lord, help me		58
— xviii. 20	Where two or three		27
— — 26 ..	And worshipped him		57
— xix. 16, 17	None good but One		28, 102
— — 26 ..	With God all things possible		112
— xx. 23 ..	Not mine to give except		102
— xxi. 9 ..	Hosanna in the highest		59
— — 44 ..	Whosoever shall fall		108
— xxii. 37, 39	Thou shalt love		13
— xxviii. 19, 20	Go ye and disciple		(note) 27, 66, 120, 151
Mark ix. 23 ..	All things possible		112
— xiii. 32 ..	Neither the Son		98, (note) 99—101
Luke ii. 40—52 ..	Childhood of Jesus		93, 99
— iii. 21, 22 ..	The heaven was opened, etc.		120, 173
— x. 16 ..	He that heareth you ..		110, 114
John i. 1—18 ..			26, 28, 45, 79, 80, 115
— ii. 19 ..	I will raise it up		103
— iii. 6—16 ..	Ye must be born again		35, 103, 173
— — ..	He that believeth		161
— iv. 10 ..	Thou wouldn't have asked		59
— v. 17—29 ..			28, 82, 101, 115
— — 30 ..	I can of myself do nothing		97 (note) 99—101
— vi. 38 ..	Not my own will		25, 96, 98
— viii. 17 ..	The testimony of two		25
— — 58 ..	Before Abraham was I am		26
— x. 14, 15 ..	The good Shepherd		28, 49, 98
— — 18 ..	No one taketh it		103
— — 30 ..	I and my Father are One		114
— — 35 ..	He called them gods ..		110, 115
— xii. 41 ..	Saw his glory and spake		53, 73
— xiv. 1 ..	Believe in God, believe in me		35
— — 6 ..	I am the way		162, 169
— — 10 ..	My Father doeth the works		97
— — 9 ..	He that hath seen me		114
— 10 ..	The Father in me		105
— — 12 ..	Greater works than these		110, 114
— 16 ..	I will pray the Father		173

			PAGE
John xiv. 21, 23 ..	We will come, etc. ..	..	66
— — 28	My Father is greater than I	..	.. 96, 101
— xv. 9	So have I loved you ..	..	.. 109, 112
— — 15	All made known to you	..	.. 110, 115
— xvi. 13	He the Spirit	..	.. 125
— xvii. 3	To know thee and Jesus Christ ..		11, 43, 96
— — 22	That they may be one	..	.. 109, 114
— — 24	Father, I will	..	.. 98
— xix. 37	Him whom they pierced	..	.. 73
— xxi. 17	Lord, thou knowest all things	..	28, 98, 152
— xx. 28	My Lord and my God	..	.. 82
Acts ii. 3	Cloven tongues of fire	..	.. 120
— — 24	Whom God raised up	..	.. 103
— v. 3, 9	Lie to the Holy Ghost	..	.. 139
— vii. 55—60	Stephen's martyrdom	..	.. 59
— ix. 14, 21 ..	All that call on thy name	..	.. 61
— — 34	Jesus Christ maketh thee whole ..		.. 104
— x. 19, 20 ..	The Spirit said, Arise, go	.:	(note) 140
— — 25, 26 ..	Stand up, I myself ..	..	.. 57
— — 36	Lord of all	..	.. 42, 75
— — 38	Holy Ghost and with power	..	(note) 137
— xiii. 2—4 ..	The Holy Ghost said, Separate ..		.. 135
— xvi. 31	Believe in the Lord Jesus	..	.. 38
— xvii. 27, 28	He is not far	..	.. 151
— xxi. 14	The will of the Lord ..	..	.. 153
— xxviii. 25 ..	Well spake the Holy Ghost	..	.. 132, 139
Romans i. 7, etc.	Grace and peace from	..	.. 69
— ii. 4—6 ..	Wrath in the day of wrath	..	14 (note) 165
— iii. 19—26 ..	.. ..		.. 169
— viii. 16	The Spirit with our spirit	..	.. 141, 174
— — 29	Firstborn among many brethren		.. 109, 113
— ix. 5	Who is over all God blessed	..	.. 83
— xiv. 10—12	We shall all stand	..	.. 46, 74
— xv. 16	Sanctified by the Holy Ghost	..	.. 153
— — 30	The love of the Spirit	..	.. 124
— xvi. 25, 26 ..	The obedience of faith	..	.. 161
1 Corinthians i. 2	All that call upon the name of Jesus		.. 60—62
— i. 2	Sanctified in Christ Jesus	..	.. 153
— ii. 1—3 ..	Nothing but Jesus Christ	..	.. 35
— — 10	The Spirit searcheth ..	..	.. 124
— — 12, 13 ..	Comparing spiritual things	..	.. 39, 143
— iii. 23	Christ is God's	..	.. 105
— viii. 6	One Lord ..	..	.. 76, 104

PAGE

1 Cor. xi. 3	The head of Christ is God		105
— xii. 11	All these worketh		123
— xiii. 12	Know even as I am known		110, 115
— xv. 24—28	Then cometh the end		106
2 Corinthians iii. 18	By the Lord, the Spirit		140
— iii. 18	The same image		109, 113
— xiii. 14	The grace of the Lord Jesus		69, 120, 174
Galatians i. 1	Paul, an apostle		68
Ephesians i. 1—7			36
— i. 17—23			103, 118
— ii. 18	Through him access		174
— iii. 8, 19	Unsearchable riches, etc		28, 41
— — 19	All the fulness of God		113, 116
— iv. 5	One Lord		76, 175
— — 8	He led captivity captive		103
— v. 5	The kingdom of Christ and God		83
— — 25	Christ gave himself		103
Philippians ii. 9—11	In the name of Jesus		46, 63
Colossians i. 15	The firstborn of all creation		(note) 105
— i. 16—18	By him were all		27, 28, 41, 105
— ii. 9	In him dwelleth		83, 116
— iii. 11	Christ is all and in all		50, 106
— — 13	Christ forgave you		104
1 Thess. i. 1	The Church in God, etc		68
— iii. 11	Now God himself		60
— — 12	The Lord make you		135
2 Thess. i. 7—9	Taking vengeance		42, 165
— ii. 13, 14	God hath chosen, etc		175
— — 16, 17	Now our Lord Jesus		60
— iii. 5	The Lord direct		135
1 Timothy ii. 5, 6	One God and One Mediator		96
Titus i.—iii.	God our Saviour, Christ our Saviour		44, 45
— ii. 10—13	Appearing of our great God		44, 84
Hebrews i. 1—12			27, 77, 106
— iv. 13	Him with whom we have to do		152
— v. 9	The author of eternal salvation		43
— ix. 14	The eternal Spirit		128, 173
— xii. 2	Author and finisher of the faith		97
James iv. 12	One lawgiver		154
— v. 20	Save a soul		110, 115
1 Peter i. 2	Elect according to		120, 175
— — 8, 9	Ye rejoice with joy unspeakable		50
— ii. 7, 8	A stone of stumbling		73

PAGE

1 Peter iv. 17	What shall the end be?	163
— — 19	To him a faithful Creator	151
2 Peter i. 1	The righteousness of our God, etc.	84
— — 4	Partakers of a Divine nature	109, 114
— — 11	The everlasting kingdom	105
— iii. 18	Doxology to Christ	50, 63
1 John i. 3	Truly our fellowship	67
— iv. 8—16	God is love	171, (note) 172
— v. 10	Believeth not the record	162
— — 20	This is the true God	43, 84
2 John 9	Whosoever transgresseth	162
Jude 1	Sanctified by God the Father	153
— 20, 21	Ye, beloved, building	175
Rev. i. 4	Seven spirits	120
— — 5, 6	Unto him that loved us	63
— — 8	I am the Almighty	28
— — 8—18	The first and the last, etc.	26, 40, 151
— ii. 23	I am he who searcheth	29, 42
— iii. 14	The beginning of the creation of God	(note) 105
— — 21	Will I grant to sit	102, 110, 114
— iv. 6	Living creatures in the midst of the throne	(note) 136
— — 8	Holy, holy, holy	138
— v. 6	Seven Spirits	106 (note) 120, 136
— — 8—14	The worship of heaven	64, 70
— xiv. 4	First-fruits unto God and to the Lamb	70
— xv. 4	Thou only art holy	152
— xix.16	King of kings and Lord of lords	41
— xxi. 22, 23	The Lord God and the Lamb	71
— xxii. 1	A pure river	106
— — 1—3	The throne of God and of the Lamb	65, 71
— — 8	I fell down to worship	58